I0413018

Rand Paul vs. Jeb Bush On The Issues

**2nd edition, April 12, 2015
Edited by Jesse Gordon,
OnTheIssues.org**

Dedication

To Ram and Lewis
who may stick with
the Paulistas this time around
and who may stick with
each other this time around

© 2015 by Jesse Gordon. All rights reserved
For reprint permission, contact
jesse@ontheissues.org
Printed in the United States of America

Rand Paul vs. Jeb Bush On the Issues

Jeb Bush and Rand Paul agree on some issues and disagree on many others. This book outlines their stances on the issues, in a side-by-side manner for each issue, on many of controversial topics that they will address in the campaign and will face as President.

We gather the two candidates' issue stances from their political biographies and memoirs; from debates in previous elections; from public speeches; from campaign websites; and from political analysis websites. All of the excerpts appear, with many additional issue stances, on our website, www.OnTheIssues.org.

Senator Rand Paul (R-KY) announced his presidential candidacy on April 7, 2015, the publication date of this book, which made him the early frontrunner because he announced early (only Senator Ted Cruz, R-TX, announced earlier, among the major Republican candidates). Governor Jeb Bush (R-FL) is always listed among the frontrunners, and the two will likely will face a large number of primary opponents. This book details the issues which Jeb Bush and Rand Paul will debate in the primaries

In general, Rand Paul represents the Tea Party and libertarian wing of the Republican Party, while Jeb Bush represents the mainstream wing. Rand already faces one Tea Party opponent in Ted Cruz; Jeb will likely face other mainstream opponents (perhaps Governor Rick Perry, R-FL). Both Jeb and Rand will also likely face a religious-right opponent (perhaps Governor Mike Huckabee, R-AR), representing the third major wing of the GOP. The 2016 Republican primary is likely to be one of the most crowded fields in recent years, with multiple candidates representing each of those three wings of the party.

This book further addresses the issues that Rand and Jeb would debate in the general election against the Democratic nominee, if either were to win the GOP primary. Rand has a well-established Senate voting record on both domestic and foreign affairs. Jeb has a well-established domestic record, but less so on foreign affairs; based on heavy research, this book presents a comprehensive outline of Jeb's foreign policy stances as of early 2015.

At this stage of the campaign, the mainstream media speculate endlessly on whether Jeb and others are running at all. We state categorically that yes, Jeb is running. He has prepared appropriately in

2014, and he has published books outlining his core campaign issues (*Immigration Wars,* by Jeb Bush, reviewed on pp. 203-6). We detail in that book review the evidence that Jeb is running.

This is the second book in our series of books about the 2016 election, and we decided to publish based on Rand's announcement date. He will release a book in June 2015 (entitled *Taking a Stand*), and Jeb will release another e-book around that same time. We decided to publish in April because Jeb's and Rand's issue stances have solidified enough that we can report them with confidence.

But won't Jeb's and Rand's issues stances change over the course of 2015? No, not likely. Candidates don't often change issue stances because then they are accused of "flip-flopping" and have to explain why they changed (for example, see how Jeb "learned" on criminal sentencing, p. 17, and how Rand "matured" on defense spending, p. 160). Of course, Jeb will develop and enunciate more specific opinions on foreign affairs over time, but we think we have captured his core values here.

Jeb's and Rand's issues stances are presented in a side-by-side format, so that you can directly compare the two, as if they debated on each topic. Sometimes we present their original words, in context, and sometimes we present some political analysis explaining the political context. Our "Notes" explain any background information required to understand the policy analysis, since politicians often speak in jargon. We also sometimes present more than one excerpt on one topic: those are intended for you to compare how the politicians have changed over time (or remained consistent over time), or to compare what the politicians *SAY* to what they *DO*. Keep it on your coffee-table for those inevitable arguments during the political season, to see what they *REALLY* mean!

The purpose of this book, and the mission of our website, is to inform voters about candidates' issue stances — what they believe about the issues, and what they have done to implement those beliefs. The mainstream media report on candidates' politics: who's ahead this week; who "won" the last debate; who has endorsed whom. We reject the "horse race politics" that dominates the mainstream media, and instead focus on what matters: Rand on the issues versus Jeb on the issues.

— Jesse Gordon, Editor-in-Chief, jesse@OnTheIssues.org
First edition: April 7, 2015
Second edition: April 12, 2015

Table of Contents

Rand Paul vs. Jeb Bush on Entitlement Issues 72

Rand Paul vs. Jeb Bush on Social Issues 106

Rand Paul vs. Jeb Bush on National Security Issues 140

Rand Paul vs. Jeb Bush

Book reviews 200

Rand Paul vs. Jeb Bush on Domestic Issues

Domestic issues focus on joint state-federal jurisdiction or joint state-federal enforcement. In the Republican primary, the Tea Party does not focus on these issues, while the libertarian wing of the Republican Party does. Libertarians agree more with Rand than they do with Jeb, on issues such as criminal prosecution, marijuana legalization, and Internet policy. Even though the Tea Party avoids domestic issues, presidential candidates seeking Tea Party support must address those issues because the national electorate demands it. This chapter includes the following sections:

- *Gun Control (pp. 12-15):* Bush and Paul follow their respective party lines on these issues: Jeb Bush supports gun rights alongside enforcement against criminal use of guns; Rand Paul supports 2nd amendment rights in the context of other constitutional rights. Jeb has been more activist on these issues, pushing Florida's "stand your ground" law; while Rand has voted against limiting ammunition clip size and is rated highly by the NRA. Any GOP debate on gun rights will focus on degree of support rather than on what the candidates support.

- *Crime (pp. 16-19):* Jeb is "tough on crime": he supports stricter sentencing and faster executions. Rand opposes harsh sentencing and questions the death penalty (i.e., he is a libertarian on crime). Jeb's tough stance invites a 4th-Amendment-oriented libertarian attack. Rand's pro-Constitution stance is part of his larger focus on welcoming minority voters to the GOP (since blacks and other minorities are disproportionately sentenced in any tough-on-crime situation).

- *Drugs (pp. 20-23):* Rand focuses on questioning the War on Drugs and on softening marijuana enforcement; Jeb supports prison for drug users and treats drugs as just another crime issue. Jeb opposes medical marijuana legalization; Rand supports decriminalization. Rand's stance on this issue is moderate compared to Ron Paul's stance (which is to abolish the Drug War and legalize marijuana); this is one of many issues where Rand is more moderate than his father. This issue is currently being addressed at the state level rather than the federal level: but the president still decides whether federal enforcement applies in states with legal pot. Jeb as president would likely undo Obama's federal non-enforcement policy, while Rand would not.

- *Infrastructure / Environment (pp. 24-31):* (including investment in environmentally-oriented infrastructure). Jeb opposes govern-ment investment in infrastructure; i.e., he considers infrastructure as another stimulus program to be avoided. Rand is less opposed, focusing on the funding sources. But neither candidate focuses much on infrastructure. Jeb did focus on hurricane recovery, which Rand opposes vehemently. Both oppose environmental spending; see economic aspects of environmental issues on pp. 56-61, and international aspects on pp. 174-179.

- *Internet / Secrecy (pp. 32-37):* Jeb and Rand view the Internet and from very different perspectives. Jeb focuses on Internet taxation and moral aspects; Rand opposes both as government intrusion. Jeb criticizes WikiLeaks while Rand criticizes the Patriot Act. This issue, which clearly differentiates these two candidates, is another area of Rand's outreach to non-traditional audiences: in this case young people who oppose federal Internet involvement.

- *Citizen Rights / Voting (pp. 38-41):* Jeb is the poster boy for less accessible voter registration, as demonstrated in his actions in 2000 (which got his brother elected President). Voting rights was a big issue in the 2014 election, with Democrats claiming that Republicans limit voting for minorities and youth, who vote heavily Democratic. Rand has stayed away from libertarian philosophy on Voter ID (libertarians oppose it), while focusing on libertarian philosophy on term limits (both support them, while Jeb benefited from term limits as governor). Also see campaign finance issues on pp. 64-65.

Rand Paul on Domestic Issues

Jeb Bush on Domestic Issues

Rand Paul on Gun Rights

Don't let the liberals tread on the Second Amendment

We are the party that adheres to the Constitution. We will not let the liberals tread on the Second Amendment! We will fight to defend the entire Bill of Rights. We will stand up against excessive government power wherever we see it. We cannot and will not allow any President to act as if he were a king. We will not let any President use executive orders to impinge on the Second Amendment.

Source: Tea Party Response to 2013 State of the Union Address, Feb. 12, 2013

Patriot Act violates your gun rights

[Speech at the Knob Creek Machine Gun Shootout, April 4, 2009]: Unless you want a government that can enter your house at will, check to see if you have trigger locks, measure the length of your guns and rapidity of their ability to fire, you must oppose violations of the Fourth Amendment like the PATRIOT Act.

Source: The Tea Party Goes to Washington, by Rand Paul, p.125, Feb. 22, 2011

NOTES: *Federal discussions on gun control often focus on the "D.C. handgun ban" because Congress has direct control over the gun laws of the District of Columbia. One such law was at issue in the case called "District of Columbia v. Heller," decided by the Supreme Court in 2008. The ruling determined that the 2nd Amendment does define an individual right to gun ownership, as opposed to a "collective right" for a state-run and state-armed National Guard. Much discretion was left to the states and to Congress, but Heller opens up the issue to further Supreme Court cases. Hence, gun control issues are still primarily the subject of Congressional legislation.*

Jeb Bush on Gun Rights

Stand-your-ground bill: Deadly force OK when threatened

In 2005, the governor signed into law another piece of NRA legislation on the topic of gun control. The bill was written by the NRA and expanded the rights of Floridians to use deadly force when threatened in public places. This proposal, known as the "stand your ground bill," expanded the rights of people to use guns or other deadly force to defend themselves without first trying to escape even in places outside their homes. The law stipulated that a person "has no duty to retreat and has the right to stand his or her ground and meet force with force, including deadly force."

The bill was opposed by police chiefs in high crime areas like Miami and Broward County who claimed it would lead "drivers with road rage or drunken sports fans who get into fights leaving ball games to assume that they had total immunity." The Brady Campaign to Prevent Gun Violence argued that it could be used to defend people who shoot in the emotional rage associated with domestic violence and other high-stress events.

Source: Aggressive Conservatism in Florida, by Robert Crew, p. 80,
Dec. 11, 2009

NOTE: *Many states have "Stand Your Ground" laws, justifying the use of deadly force when threatened, in contrast with the legal principle of an "obligation to retreat" first. The Florida version of the "stand your ground" law gained national attention in February 2012 in the case of Trayvon Martin shooting case. Martin, an unarmed black teenager, was shot and killed by a "neighborhood watch" coordinator, George Zimmerman. Citing the "stand your ground" law, Zimmerman was not initially charged, but was later arrested. He was acquitted of both murder and manslaughter in July 2013. Since then, the mainstream media report regularly on Zimmerman's new arrests & police encounters, including a "road rage" incident in Sept. 2014.*

Rand Paul on Gun Crimes

2nd amendment is only as good as the 4th amendment

How many supposed pro-gun politicians voted for the Patriot Act which gives the government the right to search your home without a warrant, when you're not home, leave listening devices, and use any and all information to create a prosecution on any charge regardless of their original reason for the search?

Gun rights advocates need to know that the 2nd amendment is only as good as the fourth amendment. If we are not free from unreasonable and warrantless searches, no one's guns are safe.

Source: Senate campaign website, www.randpaul2010.com, Sept. 1, 2010

Voted NO on banning high-capacity magazines of over 10 bullets

Congressional Summary: The term 'large capacity ammunition feeding device' means a magazine or similar device that has an overall capacity of more than 10 rounds of ammunition.

- It shall be unlawful for a person to import, sell, manufacture, or possess a large capacity ammunition feeding device.
- Shall not apply to the possession of any large capacity ammunition feeding device otherwise lawfully possessed before 2013.
- Shall not apply to qualified or retired law enforcement officers.

Source: Safe Communities, Safe Schools Act; Bill S.Amdt. 714 to S. 649 ; vote number 103 on Apr 17, 2013

NOTE: *The Newtown, Connecticut shootings in December 2012 reignited the debate on gun regulation. On December 14, 2012, Adam Lanza, 20, fatally shot twenty children and six adult staff members in a mass murder at Sandy Hook Elementary School. Several bills were proposed in the 2013-14 Congressional session: banning the sale of semi-automatic firearms, and restricting large-capacity magazines.*

Jeb Bush on Gun Crimes

Use a Gun and You're Done

During the commission of a crime:

- Pull a Gun—Mandatory 10 Years
- Pull the Trigger—Mandatory 20 Years
- Shoot Someone—25 Years to Life (whether they live or die)

New Mandatory Minimum Prison Sentences for:

- Three Time Convicted Violent Felons
- Drug Traffickers
- Aggravated Assaults/Batteries on Law Enforcement Officers or an Elderly Person
- Repeat Sexual Batterers

Source: Governor's web site, www.MyFlorida.com, "Initiatives," Nov. 7, 2001

Violent gun crime rate is down by more than 25%

Public safety has been protected, and convicted criminals will continue to serve at least 85 percent of their sentences. Over the last two years, the violent gun crime rate is down by more than 25 percent, translating into 18 fewer gun assaults each day in this state in 2000 compared to 1998.

Source: State of the State address to 2002 Florida Legislature, Jan. 22, 2002

Rand Paul on Criminal Sentencing

Blacks look who's in prison & conclude cops out to get them

Q: What about the death of Michael Brown [in a police shooting] and the unrest that followed [in ongoing riots in Ferguson, Missouri]?

PAUL: If you're African American and you live in Ferguson, the belief is, you see people in prison and they're mostly black and brown, that somehow it is racial, even if the thoughts that were going on at that time had nothing to do with race. So it's a very good chance that had this had nothing to do with race, but because of the way people were arrested, that everybody perceives it as, "My goodness, the police are out to get us," you know? I don't know what happened during the shooting, so I'm not gonna make a judgment on the shooting. But I do know what's happening, as far as that you look at who's in our prisons.

Source: Meet the Press 2014 interviews of 2016 presidential hopefuls, Aug. 24, 2014

Let convicted felons regain the right to vote

Q: You said last year "If I told you that one out of three African-American males is forbidden by law from voting, you might think I was talking about Jim Crow 50 years ago. Yet today, a third of African-American males are still prevented from voting because of the war on drugs."

PAUL: It's the biggest voting rights issue of our day. There may be a million people who are being prevented from voting from having a previous felony conviction. I'll give you an example: I have a friend who, 30 years ago, grew marijuana plants in college. He made a mistake. He still can't vote, and every time he goes to get a job he has to tick a box that says convicted felon. It prevents you from employment. We should be for letting people have the right to vote back, and I think the face of the Republican Party needs to be not about suppressing the vote, but about enhancing the vote. My bill would allow somewhere a million people to get the right to vote back.

Source: Meet the Press interview, June 22, 2014

Jeb Bush on Criminal Sentencing

1990s: punishment over therapy; 2010s: that hardens people

Bush once called for building prisons and emphasizing "punishment over therapy" for juvenile offenders. Today, he supports reforming the criminal justice system, arguing that incarceration can harden low-level lawbreakers into career criminals.

Bush "does not flip-flop," a Bush adviser said. "He learns. When he learns, he changes." Bush was particularly influenced by the experience of governing: he suddenly had access to measurements of what worked, and what did not, on issues like juvenile justice

Source: New York Times interview, "Evolving Views," Jan. 11, 2015

Ran as "tough on crime" candidate for governor

Bush's first campaign against Lawton Chiles was dominated by his efforts to appeal to the "tough on crime" constituency and to portray his opponent as "soft."

Governor Bush continued to focus support for "get tough on crime" laws. These include a variety of mandatory sentencing laws such as the 10-20-Life Act, the Three Strikes Violent Felony Offender Act, and the Habitual Offender Accountability Act, all passed in the glow of Bush's 1st-term victory. Despite evidence that the 10-20-Life law had no effect on the state's crime rate (Stoddard, 2006) Bush continued into his last year in office to cite these laws as some of the primary accomplishments of his administration.

Source: Aggressive Conservatism in Florida, by Robert Crew, p. 72-3, Dec. 11, 2009

Rand Paul on Death Penalty

We have probably executed people wrongfully

Q: Do you have concerns about the use of military drones?

PAUL: I am concerned about one person deciding the life or death of not only foreigners but US citizens around the world. And having the president decide who he's going to kill concerns me. I would rather it go through the FISA court. I mean, even in the US where we have the best due process probably in the world, we have probably executed people wrongfully for the death penalty. They have found out through DNA testing, many people on death row are there inaccurately. So I think when we decide to kill someone, that's obviously the ultimate punishment. We need to be very, very certain that what we're doing is not in error.

Source: CNN security blog interview, June 12, 2012

Death penalty is a state issue

Rand Paul said that the disproportionate number of minorities in the nation's prisons convinced him to push for sentencing reform and restoring voting rights to some convicted felons ahead of a possible presidential run in 2016. However, the fact that there are a disproportionate number of minorities on death row in the US has not led him to scrutinize capital punishment. He said the death penalty is a state issue: "I haven't had a lot of feedback specifically on that," Paul said in a phone interview. "I just haven't taken a position on the death penalty."

White people have accounted for more than half of all executions in the United States since 1976. Kentucky has executed three people since 1976—all white males—but none since 2008. The state's death penalty has been on hold since 2010 pending the outcome of a state lawsuit.

Paul said he did not know if the death penalty is an important issue to minority voters, whom he has been courting in recent months.

Source: Washington Times, July 24, 2014

Jeb Bush on Death Penalty

Fewer death-row appeals; faster executions

One of Bush's central themes during the 1994 campaign was his desire to streamline the execution process for death row inmates. He proposed limiting death row inmates to only one appeal with the state, a measure he hoped would speed up the state's execution process. Bush named his plan "one trial, one appeal," and released it in spring 1994.

Enacting the "one trial, one appeal" plan would have required Florida voters to approve an amendment to the state's constitution, but this hurdle didn't dissuade Bush. In November, he reiterated his goal, saying, "I want to accelerate, not slow down, the enforcement of the death penalty in Florida."

Source: New York Times interview, "Evolving Views," Jan. 11, 2015

Called special legislative session for death penalty law

When he miscalculated on how many votes were necessary to rewrite rules for the court system in the death penalty special session, he turned to the Republican Party's rich donors to send private [police] out to retrieve missing GOP legislators. One was dragged away from a pregnant wife on the brink of childbirth, another from his sister's funeral.

The reaction to this style of leadership varied, and was not always predictable. To many, even in the much-reviled press, Jeb was a breath of fresh air. He said what he was going to do, and then he did it, without the mealy-mouthed games that are so common among elected officials.

Source: America's Next Bush, by S.V. Dáte, p.131, Feb. 15, 2007

NOTE: *The death penalty is currently implemented in 32 states (down from 34 in 2012). It was re-legalized by a Supreme Court decision in 1977. Since then, 1,392 people have been executed. About 3,000 inmates remain on 'death Row.' Texas is by far the national leader in executions— it has executed 518 people as of November 2014, or 37% of the national total. (Oklahoma is a very distant second with 111). Florida is fourth, with 89 executions, but has 404 people on death row as of Nov. 2014 (only California has more, with 745).*

Rand Paul on War on Drugs

War on drugs has unintentionally had a racial outcome

Q: African-Americans, percentage-wise, certainly make up a larger percentage of folks being incarcerated. I think the NAACP has estimated about a third of young black males are in jail.

PAUL: Three out of four people in prison are black or brown for nonviolent drug use. However, when you do surveys, white kids are doing drugs at an equal rate, and they are a much bigger part of the population. So, why are the prisons full of black and brown kids? It is easier to arrest them. It is easier to convict them. They don't get as good of attorneys. And, frankly, they live in the city more than in the suburbs, and so the police are patrolling the city more. But it is unfair. The war on drugs has had a racial outcome, unintentionally, but it has a racial outcome. And I want to try to fix it.

Q: And your bill does change some drug laws in order to try to even out the punishment for similar drugs?

PAUL: Yes.

Source: CNN SOTU 2014 interview series, June 22, 2014

Exclude industrial hemp from definition of marijuana

Paul co-sponsored Industrial Hemp Farming Act

- Amends the Controlled Substances Act to exclude industrial hemp from the definition of "marihuana."

- Defines "industrial hemp" to mean the plant Cannabis sativa L. and any part of such plant, whether growing or not, with a delta-9 tetrahydrocannabinol concentration of not more than 0.3% on a dry weight basis.

- Deems Cannabis sativa L. to meet that concentration limit if a person grows or processes it for purposes of making industrial hemp in accordance with state law.

Source: HR1831/S3501/HR525 (2013) on Aug 2, 2012

Jeb Bush on War on Drugs

Illegal drugs moving over US-Mexico border has intensified

The movement of illegal drugs and weapons across the US-Mexican border has intensified. On the Mexican side of the border, full-scale war among paramilitary drug cartels has left 50,000 people dead over the past 6 years.

Given Mexico's inability to control the drug cartels and the massive drug market in the US, spillover effects are inevitable. The most vivid example is the horribly failed Operation Fast and Furious, in which weapons obtained from US authorities were linked to at least a dozen violent crimes in the US. Given that the cartels control an estimated 90% of the illegal drugs entering the US, their effects extend to American gangs, crime syndicates, and drug addicts.

The president should be authorized to deploy military or National Guard forces if necessary to counter the cartels' threat and secure the US border. Preferable to US military deployment would be efforts to increase the effectiveness of Mexican authorities in dealing with the cartels on their side of the border.

Source: Immigration Wars, by Jeb Bush, p. 50-53, March 5, 2013

Reduce drug use by 50% by prevention & enforcement

One of the most serious challenges our state faces is the scourge of drugs. [My drug control strategy] reflects our will and determination to reverse the years of lost human, social, and economic potential wrought by the illegal drug trade and to bring down appreciably the numbers of our citizens caught in the grip of drug abuse My administration is determined to reduce drug use in Florida by 50%. This ambitious goal can only be achieved with the commitment of our efforts and resources on many fronts-in awareness, prevention, treatment, and law enforcement.

Drug Control Strategy 1999; Introductory Letter, July 2, 1999

Rand Paul on Marijuana Legalization

Don't promote marijuana but don't jail non-violent criminals

Q: You would like to relax some of the laws for people who possess and are smoking marijuana, and synthetic recreational drugs. Why?

PAUL: The main thing I've said is not to legalize them but not to incarcerate people for extended periods of time. With Senator Leahy, we have a bill on mandatory minimums. There are people in jail for 50 years for nonviolent crimes. And that's a huge mistake. Our prisons are full of nonviolent criminals. I don't want to encourage people to do it. Marijuana takes away your incentive to work. I don't want to promote that but I also don't want to put people in jail who make the mistake. There are a lot of young people who do this and then later on, they get married and they quit; I don't want to put them in jail and ruin their lives. The last two presidents could conceivably have been put in jail for their drug use, and it would have ruined their lives. They got lucky, but a lot of poor kids, particularly in the inner city, don't get lucky.

Source: Fox News Sunday 2013 interviews, March 24, 2013

NOTE: *Marijuana is legal or partially legal in 27 states as of Nov. 2014 (up from 23 states in 2013): Alaska, Arizona, California, Colorado, Connecticut, Delaware, Hawaii, Illinois, Maine, Maryland, Massachusetts, Michigan, Minnesota, Mississippi, Montana, Nebraska, Nevada, New Hampshire, New Jersey, New Mexico, New York, North Carolina, Ohio, Oregon, Rhode Island, Vermont, Virginia, and Washington. Medical marijuana is also legal in numerous foreign countries. Medical marijuana alleviates symptoms associated with glaucoma, cancer, HIV/AIDS, and numerous mental diseases.*

Jeb Bush on Marijuana Legalization

No medical marijuana; it's just a guise toward legalization

Jeb Bush is siding with opponents of an initiative on Florida's November election ballot to make medical marijuana legal, despite strong public support for its use as a treatment for debilitating illnesses. Bush issued a statement saying the legalization of medical marijuana would hurt the state's family-friendly reputation: "Florida leaders and citizens have worked for years to make the Sunshine State a world-class location to start or run a business, a family-friendly destination for tourism and a desirable place to raise a family or retire," Bush said. "Allowing large-scale, marijuana operations to take root across Florida, under the guise of using it for medicinal purposes, runs counter to all of these efforts," he added. "I strongly urge Floridians to vote against Amendment 2 this November," he said.

Florida Governor Rick Scott signed a law in June allowing the limited use of a special non-euphoric strain of marijuana, known as Charlotte's Web. The amendment, if approved by voters, would allow marijuana to be more broadly prescribed by doctors.

Source: David Adams on Reuters: "Jeb Bush joins opposition," Aug. 14, 2014

Mandatory prison sentences for drug offenses

- Create mandatory prison sentences for persons convicted of drug trafficking.

- Mandatory minimum prison sentences of 3, 7, 15, 25 years, life or death will be imposed depending on the type and amount of the controlled substance.

- A minimum of three years will be mandated for any person convicted of possession, sale, importation, etc., of at least 25 pounds of cannabis, 4 grams of morphine, opium or heroin, or 28 grams of cocaine.

- Penalties increase as the type and amount of the drugs increase or if use of the drug results in someone's death.

Source: Governor's web site, www.MyFlorida.com, Nov. 7, 2001

Rand Paul on Transportation Infrastructure

5% tax on overseas profits & put it all into infrastructure

Q: Is there an area where you feel you can work in common cause with President Obama this year?

PAUL: You know, we make the mistake up there that we try to agree to too much. I'm the first to acknowledge the president and I don't agree on every issue, but if you took ten issues I think there are two or three that we agree on, and we agree firmly on, and why don't we go after the issues that we agree on? When I was at the White House a couple of weeks ago, I said to the president, "I want to increase infrastructure spending, and I know you do. Let's let companies bring back their profit from overseas at 5% and put it all in infrastructure." And I've been talking with Senator Durbin, others in the Senate on the Democrat side. I think we could agree to that tomorrow, but we have to go ahead and just narrow the focus and not say, "Oh, we're going to do overall tax reform," because we don't agree on overall tax reform.

Source: Meet the Press 2014 interview, Jan. 26, 2014

NOTE: *In 2008, Barack Obama backed proposed legislation for a National Infrastructure Reinvestment Bank. Obama suggested that the Bank would borrow $60 billion to invest in infrastructure over 10 years, while leveraging "up to $500 billion" of private investment. It would invest in high-speed trains to provide an alternative to air travel, energy efficiency, and clean energy, among other kinds of public infrastructure. The Bank would complement existing federal programs to fund infrastructure, such as the Highway Trust Fund or State Revolving Funds. It would invest primarily in surface transport infrastructure, which is likely to include highways, mass transit, and high-speed rail. Obama repeated the call in Sept. 2010, but no legislation resulted.*

Jeb Bush on Transportation Infrastructure

Enraged by citizen initiative mandating high speed rail

[Some] citizen initiatives absolutely enraged him: one in 2000 that mandated a high-speed rail system among the major Florida population centers. Jeb did not have a moral aversion to trains, fast or slow. [What enraged Jeb was than the] voters had passed a constitutional amendment over Jeb's objections.

The high-speed rail amendment had a champion, a longtime proponent of fast trains who happened to be a millionaire and was not afraid to take on Jeb. The proponents went to the voters to force Jeb to reconsider a decision he had made in 1999: undoing the long-standing state policy to bring high-speed rail to Florida. True, after more than a decade, the project seemed mired in endless delays.

But set aside for a moment the relative merits of keeping or canceling the bullet train. Jeb failed to understand that there was a much more reasonable way to build a consensus that high-speed rail should be terminated, than the method he chose, which was to decree this by fiat.

Source: America's Next Bush, by S.V. Dáte, p.148-149, Feb. 15, 2007

NOTE: *High-speed rail is common throughout Europe and East Asia, but has only one line in the United States, the Amtrak Acela line from Boston to New York City and Washington DC. President Obama made high-speed rail a goal in January 2009, but no projects are underway as of 2013. High-speed rail projects are proposed in California, Pennsylvania, Texas, and elsewhere. Replacing the projects canceled by Jeb Bush in 2000, a Florida high-speed rail project was approved by the Florida legislature in 2009, but canceled by Governor Rick Scott in 2011; a replacement was proposed as of 2012.*

Rand Paul on Hurricane Recovery

Hurricane recovery money is bankrupting the government

Asked Sunday about recent broadsides from New Jersey Gov. Chris Christie ("this strain of libertarianism that's going through both parties right now and making big headlines, I think, is a very dangerous thought,") and New York Rep. Peter King ("When you have Rand Paul actually comparing [Edward] Snowden to Martin Luther King, Jr., or Henry David Thoreau, this is madness."), the Kentucky senator went there: "They're precisely the same people who are unwilling to cut the spending, and their 'Gimme, gimme, gimme—give me all my Sandy money now.'" Paul said, referring to federal funding after the hurricane last year. "Those are the people who are bankrupting the government and not letting enough money be left over for national defense."

Paul said he wasn't the one itching for a fight: "I didn't start this one, and I don't plan on starting things by criticizing other Republicans," he said. "But if they want to make me the target, they will get it back in spades."

Source: Reason Magazine, July 29, 2013

NOTE: *Hurricane Katrina hit New Orleans on August 29, 2005, and breached the levies surrounding the city. Much of New Orleans was flooded, resulting in over 700 deaths and thousands of permanently lost homes. At issue politically is who was responsible for ignoring the warnings about levy breaches. Democrats blame Pres. George W. Bush, who infamously claimed about FEMA director Michael Brown, "Brownie, you're doing a heck of a job." Republicans blame Louisiana's Democratic governor and New Orleans' Democratic mayor.*

Hurricane Sandy made landfall in New Jersey, just south of New York City, on October 29, 2012. Much of the NYC metropolitan area was flooded, resulting in about 150 deaths and about $100 billion in damages. President Obama declared a state of emergency prior to landfall, part of the cautiousness resulting from Hurricane Katrina. Questions persist about whether global warming caused the intensity of Hurricane Sandy, and hence will cause future hurricanes of similar intensity.

Jeb Bush on Hurricane Recovery

2004: Universal praise for handling spate of hurricanes

Jeb drew almost universal praise for his handling of the spate of hurricanes that hit Florida in 2004. All the traits that make him such a scary leader in other areas actually work to good effect, when it comes to managing disasters. He did those things that should happen when a storm strikes. Implement an effective, thorough evacuation. And, afterward, come in quickly with massive quantities of help: search and rescue teams, water, ice, food, law enforcement—in more or less that order.

A skeptical view might see this as pure political survival: the Florida hurricanes struck a broad cross section of constituents, many if not most of them white, middle class, and Republican. This view, though, misses a key component of Jeb's personality, which is that he loves a tough challenge. He really would have responded just as vigorously if the storm had struck a predominantly black, Democratic town. Katrina serves as the perfect illustration of the difference between Jeb and Big Brother.

Source: America's Next Bush, by S.V. Dáte, p. 21-22, Feb. 15, 2007

During hurricanes, prosecutes gas stations for price gouging

In that unprecedented 2004 autumn, when 4 powerful storms slammed the state within 6 weeks, Jeb's government first immersed itself into the gasoline distribution market. One hand reached out, requesting that certain areas be given priority—even as the other closed into a fist, threatening gas station owners who price gouged with prosecution.

When asked how it could be defined as price gouging if the hurricane in question had not struck anywhere near the service station with the higher-priced gas: "I would consider it price gouging even if it's in Alaska. It's price gouging if you are raising your price, irrespective of cost, beyond a certain threshold. The same commodity, if you buy it at X and you sell if at Y for a profit, that's great. But when you take advantage of the situation and raise prices even more, I think that's price gouging." Just to make sure I was hearing this right, I asked what a reasonable profit would be on a gallon of gasoline. His answer: "2 or 3 cents."

Source: America's Next Bush, by S.V. Dáte, p.168-169, Feb. 15, 2007

Rand Paul on Environmental Protection

Our federal government regulates everything and anything

Ronald Reagan famously said, "The nine most terrifying words in the English language are, 'I'm from the government and I'm here to help.'" Three decades later, American life is micromanaged at every imaginable level. Citizens' basic day-to-day activities are subject to government scrutiny. We endure a federal government that has invaded virtually every aspect of our lives—from light bulbs, to toilets, and beyond.

Our federal government regulates everything and anything. How much water goes into you commode. How much water comes out of your showerhead. The temperature of the water in your washing machine. How many miles to the gallon your car must get.

Source: Government Bullies, by Rand Paul, p. xxiii, Sept. 12, 2012

Citizens run afoul of vague definition of "wetlands"

The Clean Water Act never even mentioned the term "wetlands" while passing through Congress for approval. The unelected bureaucracy simply created the concept and defines it in distinct terminology dependent upon whatever scenario they are currently considering. "Wetlands" quite literally can mean whatever the EPA wants it to mean.

The definition of wetlands has become so absurd that the Army Corps of Engineers developed the "migratory bird theory." This theory states that if your land is a stopping point for any migratory bird that has traveled between real navigable waters, then your land is now *de facto* connected to the interstate navigable streams. I'm not kidding.

This theory is irrational & completely illogical. How did it ever become enforceable law? It happened because Congress has abdicated its duty in this area. Citizens often run afoul of these rules inadvertently due to the constant evolution of complex and unexplained regulations.

Source: Government Bullies, by Rand Paul, p. 19-20, Sept. 12, 2012

Jeb Bush on Environmental Protection

1990s: Compensate landowners;
2010s: state-run conservation

In the past, Jeb used to emphasize the rights of big landowners who felt cheated by environmental programs. Now, he is a champion of state-sponsored conservation, celebrated for his $2 billion program to restore the Everglades. Bush insists that he will not contort himself to satisfy ideologues, but his views have already changed–in presentation, in tone, in language and, at times, in substance.

A useful case study: the environment. In 1994, Bush supported a state constitutional amendment, also backed by big corporations, to compensate landowners hurt by conservation efforts. He [supported] cutting funds to purchase environmentally fragile lands and declared that "excessive regulation does not mean we are going to improve the quality of water, air or land-use planning." But Bush met with conservation experts and toured important environmental sites across Florida. When he was elected four years later, "his heart changed," an adviser said.

Source: New York Times interview, "Evolving Views," Jan. 11, 2015

Everglades are "crown jewel" of
Florida environmental legacy

The "unwavering commitment of Governor Bush and the Florida legislature" to saving the Everglades was cited by Bush's first secretary of Environmental Protection as the "crown jewel" in Florida's environmental legacy. This legislation involved both the state of Florida and the federal government and was just the kind of big-government spending plan that Bush had deplored throughout his campaigns for office and subsequently as governor. Nevertheless, when President Clinton signed the Comprehensive Everglades Restoration Plan, Bush attended the ceremony in Washington and said, "the restoration of America's Everglades has been one of my administration's top priorities" and said later that it was *THE* highest environmental priority.

Source: Aggressive Conservatism in Florida, by Robert Crew, pp.157-8,
Dec. 11, 2009

Rand Paul on Nuclear Power

Compete on the free market, including nuclear plants

Washington's bureaucratic regulations, corporate subsidies, and excessive taxation have made it unnecessarily difficult for energy developers to take advantage of these new forms of cheap and clean energy. It also distorts the marketplace, puts the brakes on innovation, and makes it impossible for companies to know what the most efficient solutions are. Is it surprising then that energy costs are on the rise?

We should be talking about energy freedom, new technologies, and discoveries. Instead the debate in Washington continues to be about how much we should subsidize solar or ethanol, and whether we should prohibit nuclear energy or coal. We should shift the debate and cut the red tape. Like all other sectors of the economy, allowing businesses and ideas to compete on the free market will not only produce the most efficient forms of energy, but will also pass along the cost savings to the consumer.

Source: Official Senate website www.paul.senate.gov, Jan. 15, 2015

NOTE: *At issue in re-establishing construction of nuclear power plants is how to deal with the radioactive waste. Yucca Mountain is a federally-owned mountain in Nevada which the federal government has proposed as a long-term repository for nuclear waste. Yucca Mountain was selected because, in theory, it is geologically stable enough to survive intact for the thousands of years until the nuclear waste becomes harmless. The site was first proposed under Pres. Reagan in 1985-1987; Congress approved it under Pres. Bush in 2002; and then Congress canceled the program under Pres. Obama in April 2011. Lawsuits are continuing into 2015.*

Jeb Bush on Nuclear Power

Use federal funds for nuclear cleanup, with state input

Bush signed the Southern Governors' Association resolution:

- Whereas, in order to protect the health, safety and welfare of our citizens by maintaining safe and clear strategies for the transportation, disposition and environmental clean-up of the nation's nuclear materials, including nuclear weapons materials, at DOE nuclear energy and weapons complexes; now, therefore, be it

- Resolved, that the Southern Governors' Association urges Congress and the President in any national energy policy:

- provide full funding for all of DOE's past and present commitments related to clean-up operations at DOE nuclear energy and weapons complexes and disposition plans for nuclear materials, including nuclear weapons materials;

- provide full funding for all state public health and environmental sampling and analysis activities at DOE nuclear energy and weapons complexes;

- and provide clear instruction to DOE that states' rights must be respected and that plans regarding DOE sites for processing of DOE research and weapons waste must be made in consultation with the various states concluding in mutually agreeable terms.

Source: Resolution of Southern Governor's Assn. on Energy Policy on Sep 9, 2001

NOTE: *The last new nuclear plant to come on-line in the US was in 1996, due to both political and economic issues. Pres. Obama promoted new nuclear plants during as part of a comprehensive energy plan; the NRC accordingly approved a new nuclear plant design in Dec. 2011, the first in decades. Since then, construction permits have been issued to dozens of new reactors, with construction underway at five of them (this compares to 100 existing reactors at 62 different nuclear plant sites). Proponents describe this as the beginning of a "nuclear renaissance."*

Rand Paul on Internet Taxation

Voted NO on authorizing states to collect Internet sales taxes

Congressional Summary: The Marketplace Fairness Act of 2013 authorizes each state to require all sellers with sales exceeding $1 million in the preceding calendar year to collect and remit sales and use taxes, but only if complying with the minimum simplification requirements relating to the administration of such taxes & audits.

Opponent's Argument for voting No (Cnet.com): Online retailers are objecting to S.743, saying it's unreasonable to expect small businesses to comply with the detailed—and sometimes conflicting—regulations of nearly 10,000 government tax collectors. S.743 caps years of lobbying by the National Retail Federation and the Retail Industry Leaders Association, which represent big box stores. President Obama also supports the bill.

Proponent's Argument for voting Yes: (Sen. COLLINS, R-ME): This bill rectifies a fundamental unfairness in our current system. Right now, Main Street businesses have to collect sales taxes on every transaction, but because out-of-state Internet sellers don't have to charge this tax, they enjoy a price advantage over the mom-and-pop businesses. This bill would allow States to collect sales taxes on Internet sales, thereby leveling the playing field with Main Street businesses. This bill does not authorize any new or higher tax, nor does it impose an Internet tax. It simply helps ensure that taxes already owed are paid.

Opponent's Argument for voting No: (Sen. WYDEN, D-OR): This bill takes a function that is now vested in government—State tax collection—and outsources that function to small online retailers. The proponents say it is not going to be hard for small businesses to handle this—via a lot of new computer software and the like. It is, in fact, not so simple. There are more than 5,000 taxing jurisdictions in our country. Some of them give very different treatment for products and services that are almost identical.

Source: Internet Freedom Preservation Act (S.215) on Jan 9, 2007

Jeb Bush on Internet Taxation

Level playing field for Main Street vs. Internet sales tax

Bush adopted a letter to Congress from 44 Governors: "The nation's governors have a strong and unified message to Congress: deal fairly with Main Street retailers, consumers, and local governments." In a letter sent to all members of Congress late Friday, 44 governors said:

If you care about a level playing field for Main Street retail businesses and local control of states, local governments, and schools, extend the moratorium on taxing Internet access ONLY with authorization for the states to streamline and simplify the existing sales tax system. To do otherwise perpetuates a fundamental inequity and ignores a growing problem.

The current moratorium on Internet access taxes, like those consumers pay to Internet service providers, and multiple and discriminatory taxes is scheduled to expire in October. The moratorium does not apply to sales taxes.

Currently, sales and use taxes are owed on all online transactions, but states are prohibited from requiring "remote sellers" to collect and remit those levies. A 1992 US Supreme Court decision said states can only require sellers that have a physical presence in the same state as the consumer to collect so-called use taxes. In instances when a seller does not have a physical presence, consumers are required to calculate and remit the taxes owed to their home states at the end of the year. The problem is most people are unaware that they're supposed to pay, and states lack an effective enforcement mechanism. Online and catalog sellers, thereby, have a significant price advantage over Main Street businesses that must collect a sales tax on all transactions.

The loophole creates serious budget problems for schools, states, and local governments. A study estimated that states could lose as much as $14 billion by 2004 if they are unable to collect existing taxes on Web-based sales. Nearly half of state revenues come from sales taxes.

Source: NGA Press Release, "Level Playing Field" on Aug 20, 2001

Rand Paul on Net Neutrality

Long history of opposing net neutrality

Silicon Valley companies want strong rules to protect net neutrality, but Sen. Rand Paul (R-KY), who is vying to be seen as tech-friendly, is not in their corner. When asked whether he has concerns about a plan backed by President Barack Obama, which would reclassify the Internet as a utility and ban companies from charging for better Internet access, Paul said, "I don't want to see regulation of the Internet. I think it's the wrong way to go about it."

Telecom and cable companies oppose this plan, because they favor less government regulation. Net neutrality advocates argue that without regulation, these companies will force content providers to pay for faster Internet access, a move that would stifle innovation.

Paul has a history of opposing net neutrality, and his aversion to reclassifying the Internet as a utility is consistent with that. In 2011, he co-sponsored a bill to repeal net neutrality regulations adopted by the FCC. The next year, Paul backed an online manifesto that sought to block government net neutrality rules.

Net neutrality advocates fear that without FCC regulation, digital monopolies will develop, as big companies charge for Internet access. Paul said, "I don't like monopolies, but I also don't like monopolies where the government gives the monopoly. For example, in many cities, there's a virtual monopoly on cable." He pointed out, "I think if there's evidence that someone has a monopoly, let's take away government privilege that creates the monopoly."

Source: Huffington Post, "Regulation of the Internet," by Dana Liebelson, Dec. 2, 2014

Jeb Bush on Net Neutrality

Regulating the Internet is craziest ideas I've ever heard

Bush weighed in on the Federal Communications Commission's (FCC) recent move to impose utility-style rules for the Internet, which have been blasted by Republicans and major cable companies. "The idea of regulating access to the Internet with a 1934 law is one of the craziest ideas I've ever heard," he said.

The comments were the first remarks Bush had made about net neutrality, though they mirrored the opinions of other Republicans after the FCC last month reclassified broadband Internet as a "telecommunications service" similar to phone lines under the 1934 Communications Act.

Bush also echoed a common refrain that President Obama had "steamrolled" the FCC by openly endorsing the tough utility-style rules in a high profile video and through staffers' work at the White House. Republican have worried that the FCC — a legally independent agency — has lost its legitimacy due to the new Web rules. "I hope that Congress acts" to reverse the rules, Bush added.

Source: TheHill weblog, "Craziest Idea," by Julian Hattem, March 9, 2015

NOTE: *Net Neutrality is the principle behind an "open Internet": that Internet service providers may not discriminate between different kinds of online content. In the view of its proponents, Net Neutrality guarantees a level playing field for all websites and Internet technologies. Proponents of Net Neutrality include Internet content providers such as Yahoo.com, eBay.com, and Amazon.com. In the view of its opponents a free market should allow content providers to guarantee speedy delivery of their data by paying an extra fee. Opponents include hardware providers such as AT&T and Comcast, plus conservative and libertarian think tanks such as Americans for Tax Reform and the Cato Institute.*

Rand Paul on Government Secrecy

The Patriot Act is intrusive; it's what the Founders feared

Sometimes conservatives seem to believe that giving the federal government unprecedented power in spying or warrantless wiretapping is somehow a positive development, but this is exactly the sort of intrusiveness the Founders feared most. This sort of invasiveness is also precisely the reason we have a Second Amendment protecting our right to keep and bear arms.

Source: The Tea Party Goes to Washington, by Rand Paul, p. 124, Feb. 22, 2011

Snowden revealed NSA abuses, but a fair prison term is ok

Q: Is clemency for Edward Snowden [who leaked NSA files] off the table?

PAUL: I don't think we can't selectively apply the law. Edward Snowden did break a law and there is a prison sentence for that. I don't think Snowden deserves the death penalty or life in prison. I think that's inappropriate. And I think that's why he fled, because that's what he faced. Do I think that it's OK to leak secrets and give up national secrets and things that could endanger lives? I don't think that's OK, either. But I think the courts are now saying that what he revealed was something the government was doing was illegal.

Q: So no clemency for Edward Snowden, but perhaps leniency?

PAUL: Well, I think the only way he's coming home is if someone would offer him a fair trial with a reasonable sentence. I think, really, in the end, history is going to judge that he revealed great abuses of our government and great abuses of our intelligence community.

Source: ABC This Week, Jan. 11, 2014

Jeb Bush on Government Secrecy

WikiLeaks is abhorrent but showed seriousness of Iran threat

Bush commented on the heels of a disclosure of secret U.S. diplomatic communications made by WikiLeaks. Several documents indicated that Arab states, including Saudi Arabia, had pressed the U.S. to bomb Iran.

Bush called the latest WikiLeaks disclosure of tens of thousands of confidential diplomatic cables "abhorrent" and "absolutely disgusting." But the Florida Republican said the content of the cables do reveal the true source of the ongoing instability roiling the Middle East.

"It does show that Iran poses the greatest threat in the region, when countries that publicly say Israel is the greatest threat, privately say the obvious, which is that Iran is the greatest threat," Bush told Newsmax. "It should bring home the fact that this should be a higher priority in terms of our own foreign policy." Bush also said sanctions against Iran, whose nuclear-arms program he termed "a huge threat," should be further strengthened as well.

Source: David A. Patten and Kathleen Walter on Newsmax.com, Nov. 29, 2010

NOTES: *From 2006 to 2013, WikiLeaks posted more than 250,000 classified documents online. The documents offered an unprecedented look at the American diplomatic process—and most well-known, in April 2010 releasing a video documenting a war crime by U.S. forces in Baghdad (obtained from Pfc. Bradley Manning, who in 2013 was sentenced to 35 years in prison for disclosing the classified video). WikiLeaks' Julian Assange is a hero to progressives who believe in open government and oppose secrecy, but a traitor to many others.*

The progressive hero / traitor mantle passed to Edward Snowden in March 2013, with the release of over 100,000 documents from the National Security Agency (NSA), exposing a massive program of domestic surveillance of U.S. citizens. When the U.S. government filed charges, Snowden fled to Russia, where he is seeking asylum in Latin America. As with Julian Assange, opponents claim that Snowden breached national security; supporters claim Snowden exposed illegal federal activities.

Rand Paul on Term Limits

Instead of bringing home the bacon, bring home politicians

"We are bankrupting this country, and the bottom line is that the politicians don't get it. The only message they will understand is a one-way ticket home. Instead of bringing home the bacon, let's bring home the politicians. Bring them home to live with the mess they've created."

I ended my speech that day with one simple line: "I'm Rand Paul and I approve this message."

Source: The Tea Party Goes to Washington, by Rand Paul, pp. 9-10, Feb 22, 2011

Term limits would infuse Congress with new ideas

All is not well in America. America is adrift. Something is clearly wrong. America needs many things, but what America desperately needs is new leadership.

There is no monopoly on knowledge in Washington. The best thing that could happen is for us—to once and for all—limit the terms of all politicians. We already limit the President to two terms. I think we should put limits on the terms of Congress and infuse our government with fresh ideas.

Source: Tea Party response to the 2015 State of the Union address, Jan 20, 2015

Jeb Bush on Term Limits

Legislative term limits strengthened Bush's executive power

Term limits were enacted in Florida in 1992 and, by a stroke of good fortune for the governor, became effective just as Bush took office, forcing out of the 2000 legislature more than half of the experienced members. This change had an effect similar to that in other states, emptying the legislature of experience and forcing green legislators to struggle with issues so complex that by the time they began to understand them, it was time for them to leave.

Throughout history, the state legislature has been viewed as the dominant political institution in Florida and in the 1980s was described as one of the strongest legislatures in the nation. Within a few years of Bush taking office, this dominance was reversed. The transformation was aided by term limits. Lobbyists and the executive office were the real winners in this environment and term limits gave Bush additional influence over the legislature.

Source: Aggressive Conservatism in Florida, by Robert Crew,
pp. 19 & 64-5, Dec. 11, 2009

NOTES: *The Constitution limits the president to two terms, or a total of 10 years. There are not limits for the US House or the US Senate.*

In March 1998, the Supreme Court let stand term limits for state lawmakers, but previously ruled that establishing such restrictions nationally would require amending the Constitution. Efforts to limit federal Congressional terms died out in early 1997. Eighteen states have laws limiting politicians' terms, and in 1998, more than 200 state legislators were forced to retire.

The latest push is for term limits for judges. The purpose would be to limit 'Judicial activism,' which means establishing new laws from the bench rather than from Congress.

Rand Paul on Voter Registration

Supports early voting; but voter ID also ok

Q: what about this business about tightening up the voter I.D. laws? Should they be tighter? Should they have to show all this identification?

PAUL: I have mixed feelings. When I go in a government building, I have got to show my driver's license. So, I am not really opposed to it. I am opposed to it as a campaign theme. If you want to get the African-American vote, they think that this is suppression somehow and it's a terrible thing. I really think that we should restore the voting rights of those who had a previous conviction; that's where the real voting problem is. I'm not against early voting. I grew in Texas. We voted early for a month or two before elections for probably 20 years, and Texas is still a Republican state. But it's perception. The Republicans have to get beyond this perception that they don't want African-Americans to vote. Now, I don't think it's true. I'm not saying it's true. But by being for all these things, it reinforces a stereotype that we need to break down.

Source: Face the Nation interview, Nov. 2, 2014

NOTES: *The voter registration issue has been brewing since 2000, and may result in legislation prior to the 2016 election. Republicans favor "Voter Identification" requirements, on the grounds of ensuring the integrity of the vote. Democrats respond that individual fraud is extremely rare and has not ever affected an election outcome. The partisan reason for these stances is that voter identification discourages voting by youth, minorities, and the elderly, all of whom disproportionately favor Democrats. In general, Jeb opposes more open voter registration, while Rand has mixed opinions (because one of his major constituencies, young voters, would most benefit from early voting).*

Jeb Bush on Voter Registration

Scrubbed voter registration rolls to eliminate felons

Just as he had in 2000, Gov. Bush pushed ahead with an aggressive scrubbing of the voter registration rolls to eliminate felons, who under a dated, Jim Crow-era state law cannot regain their right to vote unless they first undergo a tedious clemency process. Needless to say, a disproportionate number of the felons are black, and blacks disproportionately vote for Democrats.

Jeb not only defended the creation of the list, but also the clearly unconstitutional law that prevented the list from being released as a public record. It took a lawsuit by CNN to get the matter before a judge— who needed about 5 seconds to declare the law unconstitutional and order Jeb to turn over the master voter roll to anybody who wanted it. And it took about 5 days for reporters to notice that there was something unusual about the felon list: it included virtually no Hispanics. Of course, Florida Hispanics tend to vote disproportionately for Republicans, but Jeb and his people said that that had nothing to do with the glitch.

Source: America's Next Bush, by S.V. Dáte, p.123-124, Feb. 15, 2007

No conspiracy of hackers manipulating electronic voting

After the 2000 election, Jeb Bush promised to replace much of the state's hated voting technology, including Palm Beach County's butterfly ballots along with their notorious hanging chads.

The new system the counties chose was touch-screen voting machines. But that didn't work out too well. The costs were high. The glitches were constant. And worst of all, no one seemed to trust the electronic counts. Without paper records, how did voters know their choices were being accurately recorded? How could anyone be sure some evil hacker wasn't manipulating the results? Jeb dismissed those fears as "conspiracy theories." But in the run-up to the 2004 presidential election, the Republican Party of Florida sent out fliers urging their voters to use absentee ballots because of the disturbing absence of a paper trail from the Election Day machines.

Source: The Party's Over, by Gov. Charlie Crist, p. 92, Feb. 4, 2014

Rand Paul vs. Jeb Bush on Economic Issues

Economic issues focus on the recession recovery and all fiscal matters. Jeb and Rand both follow the mainstream Republican Party opinions on these issues, but Jeb is more moderate and willing to compromise on economic issues (but Rand will seem moderate compared to some other likely primary opponents who are even more hard-core anti-tax-and-spend conservatives). This chapter includes the following sections:

- *Corporations (pp. 46-51):* Both Rand and Jeb say they oppose corporate welfare, but both their critics say they encourage corporate welfare. Rand's opposition to the federal bank bailout (which Jeb supported) makes Rand's anti-corporate welfare stance somewhat more believable, but they both support corporate tax cuts. Neither makes corporate issues a major focus of their policies.

- *Budget & Economy (pp. 52-55):* Jeb and Rand differ strongly on earmarks: Jeb supports (like most mainstream candidates) and Rand opposes (like most libertarian and Tea Party candidates). Both oppose earmarks, which are certain to be a hot issue in the 2016 Republican primary (Republican Senate Majority Leader Mitch McConnell, R-KY, is the strongest proponent *for* earmarks). The biggest issue for 2016 is how to extend (or terminate) the Great Recession programs for the post-Recession period; both Rand and Jeb agree on reducing deficit spending, but Rand would mandate a balanced budget, while Jeb would work with Democrats to reduce the deficit.

- *Economic aspects of energy & environment (pp. 56-61):* Rand Paul opposes EPA action so strongly that he wrote a book about it (*Government Bullies*, book review on p. 207). Rand considers EPA action to be federal over-reach, applied both to energy exploration as well as environmental protection. Jeb does respect environmental protection (see Jeb's Everglades defense, p. 29), but Jeb and just about all Republicans greatly disrespect "green energy." Jeb claims that green energy is a form of "crony capitalism," i.e. that it is just another federal program that provides an excuse to enrich Democratically-favored industries, but is more moderate than many in the GOP. Jeb treats offshore drilling as an environmental protection issue, and hence mostly opposes it, unlike most Republicans, who support it along with Rand Paul. See international aspects of environmental issues on pp. 174-179, and infrastructure aspects on pp. 24-31.

- *Government Reform (pp. 62-65):* On the policy side, this section focuses on the size of the federal government, which Jeb thinks should be more privatized, while Rand prefers audits (in contrast to Ron Paul's preference for abolishing federal agencies). On the political side, Rand would restrict campaign financing by PACs, while Jeb would loosen campaign finance. The 2016 campaign will be the first run under the new *Citizens United* unlimited PAC money rules. Also see voting issues on pp. 38-41.

- *Tax Reform (pp. 66-71):* including income taxes, tax rates, and bracket redistribution. Both Rand and Jeb would reduce corporate taxes and inheritance taxes, which is the mainstream Republican view. But Jeb Bush differs from many Republicans by declining the "No New Taxes" pledge that Rand Paul and many GOP candidates have signed. Jeb's father, the senior George Bush, famously broke his no-new-taxes pledge, and Jeb's compromising attitude on taxes means he will likely be challenged on this issues by Rand other economically conservative primary opponents.

Rand Paul on Economic Issues

Jeb Bush on Economic Issues

Rand Paul on Corporate Regulation

Punishing the rich means the poor lose their jobs

Mr. President, you say the rich must pay their fair share. When you seek to punish the rich, the jobs that are lost are those of the poor and middle class.

When you seek to punish Mr. Exxon-Mobil, you punish the secretary who owns Exxon Mobil stock.

When you block the Keystone Pipeline, you punish the welder who works on the pipeline.

Source: Republican National Convention speech, Aug. 29, 2012

Obama's "You didn't build that" insults American workers

When I heard the current president say, "You didn't build that," I was first insulted, then I was angered, then I was saddened that anyone in our country, much less the president, believes that roads create business success and not the other way around.

The great and abiding lesson of American history, particularly the Cold War, is that the engine of capitalism—the individual—is mightier than any collective. American inventiveness and desire to build developed because we were guaranteed the right to own our success. For most of our history, no one dared tell Americans: "You didn't build that."

When you say they didn't build it, you insult each and every American who ever got up at the crack of dawn. When the president says, "You didn't build that," he is flat out wrong. Businessmen and women did build that. Businessmen and women did earn their success. Without the success of American business, we wouldn't have any roads, or bridges, or schools.

Source: Republican National Convention speech, Aug. 29, 2012

Jeb Bush on Corporate Regulation

Champion enterprise zones and business deregulation

The past four years have not been kind to small businesses. Republicans should bring their message of low taxes and moderate regulatory policies to Hispanic communities whose economic future depends on such policies.

In particular, licensing regulations often disproportionately hamper Hispanic businesses that tend to operate informally. Republicans should champion enterprise zones, deregulation of entry into occupations and businesses that require few skills and little capital, and lower business taxes. More important, they should engage Hispanic business and community leaders in identifying & eradicating barriers to enterprise. As Democrats continue compounding the inherent risks of small businesses by piling on taxes & regulations at every level of government, Republicans should be seen as ardent defenders of small businesses.

Source: Immigration Wars, by Jeb Bush, p.216, March 5, 2013

NOTES: *The federal government "bailed out" the Big Three automakers early in the 2008 Great Recession. The bailout consisted of direct loans to General Motors and Chrysler, and a line of credit for Ford Motors. President Bush's loan to GM and Chrysler (originally $17 billion and ultimately $64 billion) was contingent upon the two automakers following federal government restructuring of their companies, and later improving fuel efficiency standards. The purpose of the bailout was to avoid bankruptcy and a large surge in unemployment of auto workers. It was criticized (mostly by Republicans) as "government intervention."*

The U.S. Treasury sold its last GM stock from the bailout loan in December 2013, repaying taxpayers $39 billion out of the total $50 billion invested (a 20% loss). When Chrysler stock was sold in 2011, taxpayers were repaid $11.1 billion out of a $12.4 billion (a 10% loss). Ford received a $5.9 billion loan in 2009, which is still being repaid. In theory, six million jobs were saved.

Rand Paul on Corporate Welfare

Stop subsidizing profitable large multinational corporations

Sen. Paul took to the Senate floor to introduce amendments that would reduce the scope, power, and corporate welfare functions of the Export-Import Bank. These amendments would essentially bring an end to the US government subsidizing loans to multinational corporations with taxpayer dollars.

TRANSCRIPT: I rise today in opposition to corporate welfare. At a time when our country is borrowing over a trillion dollars a year, I think it makes no sense to loan money back to countries we are borrowing from. For example, we borrowed $29 billion from Mexico, and yet we're sending them back $8 billion of the money we borrow from them to subsidize trade. A lot of the subsidized trade goes to very wealthy corporations. We're not talking about starting new companies; we're mostly talking about subsidizing very wealthy multinational companies. With the start-up companies the export-import bank is subsidizing [companies that donate to federal officials and Obama].

Source: Senate press release, "Subsidizing MNCs," March 20, 2012

No safety net cuts until corporate welfare is all cut

I believe we should do the opposite. I propose we cut everyone's taxes, from the richest to poorest, and we cut spending at the same time. Imagine a private stimulus fed by allowing you to keep more of your own money! Some will ask, "But what of the safety net?" I say: We will not cut one penny from the safety net until we've cut every penny from corporate welfare! So much of Washington's inability to cut waste in government comes from them not doing their job. It has been several decades since Congress passed all the spending bills individually. Instead, the spending bills are lumped together in something that is thousands of pages long. They allow no amendments to cut wasteful spending. Often the bill is plopped on our desk with only a few hours to review. No one, and I mean no one, is able to read what is in the bill. To fix this, I will introduce legislation called "Read the Bills Act." It mandates that Congress wait one day for each 20 pages of legislation.

Source: Tea Party response to the State of the Union, Jan. 20, 2015

Jeb Bush on Corporate Welfare

Fight corporate welfare: snouts out of public trough

Responsibility and self-government [also apply to] programs that are considered by many to be corporate welfare. Limited government does not mean limited for only one portion of society, one economic class. We cannot ask government to do less for the many while doing more for the few. Limited government is about the fair distribution of limited resources, meaning that as we criticize social spending for being no solution to our social problems, we should also criticize unnecessary corporate entitlements as no cure for our competitiveness problems. Creating barriers to competition and sanctuaries for profit is no answer. Many industries realize that they profit from a bigger, more involved government. Yet a return to limited self-government would not be complete without pushing these corporate snouts out of the public trough. Limiting the role of government must be a process that is rational, equitable, and principled.

Source: Profiles in Character, by Jeb Bush, p.172-173, Nov. 1, 1995

Stop rewarding portfolio Americans over paycheck Americans

In order to spur the economy, Bush said ObamaCare needs to be repealed. "Our current policy rewards portfolio Americans at the expense of paycheck America while enabling the greatest sustained deficits in American history," Bush said. "Conservatives need to advance economic freedom by working to repeal ObamaCare and replacing it with a system that is consumer-directed, less coercive and significantly less costly."

Source: Tal Kopan on Politico.com, "Crony Capitalism," Oct. 29, 2013

Rand Paul on Recession Bailout

Bank bailout represented everything wrong with Washington

A vote for the bank bailout bill was wrong for many reasons—and particularly the way it was passed—1,000 pages long, printed at midnight and passed by noon the next day. No one read the bill. It came out of the shadows and was passed in the midst of a government-created crisis, featuring new regulations and new powers for government, inserted into its crevices by anonymous clerks in the dead of night. The bank bailout represented everything that was wrong with Washington.

My father, a Congressman, told me that he had banking lobbyists calling him and asking him about certain sections of the boll, and he said, "What bill?" He didn't have a copy yet. They replied, "We do, would you like to see it?" You know government is out of control when lobbyists have the bills before members of Congress. Who is writing the bills, Congress or the lobbyists?

Source: The Tea Party Goes to Washington, by Rand Paul, p. 49-50, Feb 22, 2011

The sequester is the law of the land: can't compromise on it

Q: Do you have a bottom line below which you will not go in accepting something that would end this standoff?

PAUL: I'm willing to compromise. But we're borrowing more than a million dollars every minute. So, we do have to address that. I think the one thing I cannot accept is the Democrats want to exceed the sequester caps, these things that we put into law to restrain spending already. And it's funny, they're all about ObamaCare being the law of the land, but so is the sequester. The sequester is the law of the land, and if we exceed that, it's a real big step in the wrong direction.

Q: The sequester means forced budget cuts that unless there is some agreement on Capitol Hill about spending, they go into place.

PAUL: Yes, and to clarify what the sequester cuts are, they're a cut in the rate of increase of spending, because over ten years, even with the sequester, government will grow over 10 years.

Source: CNN SOTU interview, Oct. 13, 2013

Jeb Bush on Recession Bailout

Bank bailouts were needed to avoid financial unraveling

Q: Should McCain have opposed the bailout?

A: I don't know. Maybe if he had opposed the bailout based on some actual principles he could express, that would have shown leadership.

Q: You have defended the early bailouts, those implemented by your brother?

A: If there wasn't any support, given the intricate nature of all these credit-default swaps, you could have had an unraveling of the financial system. So I'm not sure there was another choice. There may have been a different means of doing it.

Source: Tucker Carlson interview of Jeb Bush in Esquire, Aug. 1, 2009

Auto bailout was government intervening; bank bailout was ok

Former Florida Gov. Jeb Bush was invited to speak to the House Budget Committee by the committee's chairman, Rep. Paul Ryan, R-Wisc., author of a federal budget despised by Democrats in part for its proposed changes to the Medicare program for seniors. Bush's remarks focused on removing barriers to free enterprise, but throughout the hearing, he was free with his opinions on all sorts of other policy matters.

Bush said that until the hearing, he hadn't been asked his opinion on the automotive bailout or the bank bailouts. He told the committee he didn't support the auto bailout—what he describes as "a form of capitalism where the government intervenes in a very muscular kind of way." The positions puts him in line with Romney. Bush did say, however, say that he thought some aspects of the bank bailout were necessary.

Source: Tampa Bay Times, "Jeb Bush cools VP chatter," June 1, 2012

Rand Paul on Budget Deficit

We borrow $1M per minute; mandate a balanced budget

It is self-evident that the President and Congress are unable to do what every family in America must do—balance the budget. If Congress cannot, or will not, balance the budget, then we should amend the Constitution to make it mandatory. President Obama is on course to add more to our national debt than all previous presidents combined. We borrow a million dollars a minute. Our $18 trillion dollar debt has become an anchor. Some economists argue that the burden of debt costs us a million jobs a year.

I fear that this enormous burden of debt threatens our currency. I fear that another 2008-style panic is possible, and I fear that this degree of debt is an imminent threat to our national security.

You cannot project power from bankruptcy court. It does not make us appear stronger when we borrow money from China and send it to countries that burn our flag.

Source: Tea Party response to the 2015 State of the Union address, Jan. 20, 2015

NOTE: Spending totals in FY2015's $3.8 trillion budget:
- ***Non-discretionary spending:***
- *$897 billion (23%) Social Security payments*
- *$860 billion (23%) Medicare/Medicaid/SCHIP payments*
- *$251 billion (7%) interest on the National Debt*
- *$659 billion (17%) other 'mandatory' payments*
-
- ***Discretionary spending:***
- *$606 billion (16%) national defense*
- *$543 billion (14%) other 'discretionary spending'*

When politicians discuss cutting "non-discretionary non-defense" spending, they are focusing on only 14% of the budget, and really mean "don't cut spending." The Sequester cuts the budget across-the-board and hence is described as cutting mostly entitlements and defense, which is true because entitlements and defense are most of the budget.

Jeb Bush on Budget Deficit

Bipartisan compromise to reduce the deficit significantly

Jeb Bush seems to be bucking the trend. He is seeking to return the party to its ideological moorings—toward the centrism of his grandfather. Even before the GOP's ignominious defeat in November, Jeb was offering tough love to his party, suggesting that Republicans stand up to Grover Norquist and craft a bipartisan compromise to reduce the deficit significantly. But will Republicans listen? There are many reasons to believe they won't.

Hence, in evaluating Jeb's prescriptions for fiscal responsibility, today's Republicans should recall the Bushes' past political palm reading. While Jeb's prescriptions are in the party's long-term interest, they will be difficult to execute, given the strength of the party's coalition members.

Can Jeb sway a resistant party base? It's quite possible: His family's odyssey has reflected the party's shifts for 50 years, and he's uniquely positioned to convince his peers.

Source: Jeff Smith, CNN Opinion, "Sway the GOP on taxes," Dec. 11, 2012

*NOTE: The annual budget deficits don't get paid off each year—they just accumulate year after year, into the National Debt, which is currently at $17.9 trillion as of the end of 2014. The 2015 budget includes a deficit of $565 billion (more spending than revenue). We pay interest in that debt—amounting to $251 billion in Fiscal Year 2015. Congress determines the "**debt ceiling**," which is the total amount that the federal government can be in debt. The actual debt must remain lower than the "debt ceiling" or the government may not borrow more money.*

*The "**fiscal cliff**" refers to the set of policy changes that took place on Jan. 1, 2013, including the expiration of the Bush tax cuts; the implementation of the "**sequester**" (across-the-board spending cuts); and the raising of the national debt borrowing limit. Alarmists claim that allowing the current policy set will send the US back into recession, hence the alarmist metaphor of "going over the cliff".*

Rand Paul on Earmarks

Our legislative victory: an end to earmarks

A significant target of voter outrage has been the practice of earmarking, a long-standing Washington method of tacking on pork-barrel spending to just about any piece of legislation. After the 2010 elections, enough new leaders had been elected who wanted to change business as usual in government. By the end of the year, we finally had a major legislative victory on this important issue—and we put an end to earmarks.

Within a month after the elections, even President Obama was hearing the message. In his State of the Union speech, President Obama embraced the era of no earmarks. I joked that instead of Washington co-opting the Tea Party, we were co-opting Washington. The Tea Party was even co-opting President Obama!

Source: Now Or Never, by Sen. Jim DeMint, p. xi-xii, Jan. 10, 2012

No Pork Pledge: decrease earmarking; increase transparency

Paul signed Citizens Against Government Waste's "No Pork Pledge": Despite congressional reforms over the past several years to reduce pork barreling and increase earmark accountability and transparency, earmarks continue to figure prominently as the "currency of corruption" on Capitol Hill, undermining the federal budgetary process and our democratic system of government. Incumbents and candidates vow not to request any pork-barrel earmark, which is defined as meeting one of the following criteria:

- Requested by only one chamber of Congress
- Not specifically authorized
- Not competitively awarded
- Not requested by the President
- Greatly exceeds the President's budget request or the previous year's funding
- Not the subject of congressional hearings
- Serves only a local or special interest

Source: Citizens Against Government Waste's "No Pork Pledge"
on Aug 12, 2010

Jeb Bush on Earmarks

Vetoed more than $2.3 billion in earmarks

Former Florida Governor Jeb Bush spoke before attendees of the Mortgage Bankers Association conference in Chicago. He advised advocacy: "Advocate and persuade. There is real hostility toward business in Washington. There's not a lot of love. In those kinds of circumstances, most business organizations go into a fetal position. That doesn't work," he said. Bush spoke against turning a blind eye, and instead encouraged proactivity.

"The problem that got us into this mess was the real estate problem, but there is very little going on to solve the real estate problems," he said. "Who better to advocate a policy to get us out of this mess? Why not defend your positions in the marketplace of ideas? Business has gotten way too timid. The natural inclination is to cower. I would encourage you to stand up."

Source: Elizabeth Ecker in Reverse Mortgage Daily, Oct. 12, 2011

NOTE: "Earmark Reform" refers to changing the rules of Congress to restrict "earmarks," which are currently legal and considered ethical.

- *"Earmarks" means line items in legislative bills which allocate specific monetary resources to a specific purpose (or to a specific company).*

- *An example is a highway improvement project in a House member's district, buried in a 1,000-page spending bill.*

- *Earmarks have become controversial because, in theory, members of Congress could quietly allocate an earmark that would benefit a campaign donor (known as "pork-barrel spending").*

- *Proposed reforms range from full disclosure (showing every earmark and its originating legislator on a public website) to the Line Item Veto (allowing the President to veto earmarks without vetoing the entire spending bill).*

Rand Paul on Environment vs. Economy

EPA regulations cost $15 trillion in 2012

Since its creation in 1970, the Environmental Protection Agency has done more harm than good. EPA regulations cost more than 5% of our annual gross domestic product (which was over $15 trillion in 2012). This is equivalent to the costs of defense and homeland security combined. Most Americans are unaware of this.

Too often our rights are violated by abusive and power-hungry EPA bureaucrats who use threats, coercion, and force to implement power grabs. I wish these instances of abuse were random and the exception, but they have unfortunately come to characterize what many Americans now rightly see as a rogue government agency. EPA regulations have hampered landowners' ability to manage their private property as they please and have seriously impaired job creation. As with the massive cost of the EPA, many Americans are unaware of the routine suffering caused by the overreach of such regulatory agencies.

Source: Government Bullies, by Rand Paul, p. 5-6, Sept. 12, 2012

EPA enforcement nullifies due process and judicial review

[The Sacketts were building their own home when the EPA ordered them to stop]. They requested a hearing before the EPA where they could challenge the agency's claim that their property was a wetland. The EPA refused, claiming property owners have no right to a hearing regarding compliance orders. Throughout this waiting process, the daily $75,000 fine continued to accumulate.

However, they filed their own lawsuit in federal court, arguing that the Administrative Procedure Act entitled them to a hearing before a judge. Yet the Sixth and Fourth Circuits rejected any possibility of judicial review. Is this not a complete violation of the separation-of-powers principle? These circuit courts essentially handed the EPA free rein over innocent Americans and their private property. Our government was literally telling the Sacketts that in the US, you are free—unless the EPA decides to get involved, at which point your right to due process and private property becomes null and void.

Source: Government Bullies, by Rand Paul, p. 35-36, Sept. 12, 2012

Jeb Bush on Environment vs. Economy

Restrict Eminent Domain;
most severe of all government powers

The power of government to take property is perhaps the most severe of all governmental powers. State government must be frugal in the exercise of this power, and conscientious when it is expanded.

In this particular bill, eminent domain authority is expanded to benefit the North Broward Hospital District. This is undoubtedly a worthwhile and needed project, [and] the hospital has begun negotiations with local property owners to purchase their properties.

My objection to this well-intended bill, however, is that the hospital has begun this process [under the old rules, and] to change these rules [in the middle of the process] would not be in the spirit of fair play.

Additionally, this bill would set a dangerous precedent for one-time expansions of eminent domain authority. I believe this is a poor basis for creating new statutes. If the expansion of quick-take authority is an issue that needs addressing, the Legislature should do so as a policy debate for statewide application.

Source: Approval notification on Senate Bill 1230, June 7, 2000

Let industries "self-audit"; compensate for "takings"

Supports the following principles concerning the environment:

- Support "self-audit" legislation which creates incentives for industries to audit themselves and clean up pollution

- Require full compensation when environmental regulations limit uses on privately owned land

- Request added flexibility from the federal government in enforcing and funding federal environmental regulations

- Supports extending the Preservation 2000 program in Florida.

Source: Florida National Political Awareness Test, July 2, 1998

Rand Paul on Oil Drilling

Supports Keystone XL, plus domestic oil & gas exploration

My plan would also approve the construction of the Keystone XL pipeline. I have consistently and repeatedly voted to allow this project to proceed. Rather than create thousands of new jobs, expand America's refining capacity, and strengthen our unique partnership with neighboring Canada, President Obama has elected instead to block any progress on building the Keystone XL, in stark contrast to the "all-of-the-above" approach to energy production he claims to support.

By allowing domestic oil, gas and mining exploration to proceed while encouraging the competitive development of alternative, renewable energy sources, I believe that the principles I have set forth in my budget plan are a significant improvement over the Obama Administration's hostile approach to traditional energy development. As a U.S. Senator, I am committed to doing what is not only best for the Commonwealth of Kentucky, but also the United States as a whole in developing a sound energy policy.

Source: official Senate website www.paul.senate.gov, Jan. 15, 2015

NOTE: The Keystone Pipeline project brings oil from Canada through eight states to refineries in Illinois and Texas. The Keystone XL is a proposed shortcut (through Montana instead of North Dakota), which would shorten the route and increase capacity. The Keystone pipeline itself was completed in 2014; the Keystone XL expansion was passed by Congress in early 2015. President Obama vetoed Keystone XL because the new route passed through an environmentally-sensitive area in Nebraska.

NOTE: Drilling for oil off the Outer Continental Shelf (OCS), several miles offshore is currently controlled by States in waters up to three miles offshore; the federal government controls waters from that distance until the continental shelf ends and the deep ocean begins (a maximum of about 350 miles offshore). Conservatives favor OCS drilling to reach more potential oil reserves; liberals cite the greater technical challenges and the higher risk of oil spills. Jeb attempts to compromise between the two viewpoints, by restricting drilling in state waters and some federal waters.

Jeb Bush on Oil Drilling

Drilling in Gulf of Mexico hurts Florida tourism industry

The Interior Department faces opposition from Jeb Bush to its proposal to auction off rights to a six-million-acre field in the Gulf of Mexico. "I am confident," Governor Bush wrote in a letter to the secretary of the interior, "that the new administration will recognize the need to protect sensitive natural resources located both offshore and along Florida's coastline for the benefit of the entire nation."

The area that Jeb Bush seeks to stop from being auctioned is not covered by the existing moratorium [on other off-shore drilling]. It actually lies off the coast of Alabama, but close enough to Florida to worry state environmentalists. "Florida's economy is based upon tourism and other activities that depend on a clean and healthy environment," Jeb Bush wrote in his letter to Washington. "As a result, we have the nation's best beaches, abundant fisheries, and pristine marine waters. Protection of those resources is of paramount importance to the state of Florida."

Source: David Sanger, NY Times, p. A17, Jan. 25, 2001

2005: 125-mile no-drill zone; then 75 miles ok for drilling

In 2001, Jeb trumpeted the deal he had won to back off federal plans to permit drilling in the Eastern Gulf: a new drilling moratorium that he proclaimed would protect Florida's beaches, a major source of the state's top industry, tourism: "As a result, there will be no new drilling in the Lease Sale 181 Area under my watch," Jeb announced.

In 2005, Jeb was ready to deal away half of that protected water. Instead of preventing drilling anywhere in a 200-mile-wide strip around Florida—the entire extent of the US's economic zone—Jeb was ready to give up the outer 75 miles of that in exchange for a permanent 125-mile zone that would be under state control.

Jeb argued that higher oil and gas prices made Florida's outright ban untenable—Jeb suggested acidly that he could take up such an idea with his fairy godmother—and that a permanent ban of any kind was better than a series of moratoria that could eventually end.

Source: America's Next Bush, by S.V. Dáte, p.365-366, Feb. 15, 2007

Rand Paul on Renewable Energy

Supports renewable energy tax credits

The Christian Coalition voter guide is one of the most powerful tools Christians have ever had to impact our society during elections. This simple tool has helped educate tens of millions of citizens across this nation as to where candidates for public office stand on key faith and family issues. The CC survey summarizes candidate stances on the following topic: "Tax credits for investment in renewable sources of energy, (such as wind, solar & biomass)"; Rand Paul was summarized as "Support."

Source: Christian Coalition Survey on Aug 11, 2010

Supports all-of-the-above energy policy

Paul signed the *Contract From America* [which includes]:

- *Pass an 'All-of-the-Above' Energy Policy:*

- Authorize the exploration of proven energy reserves to reduce our dependence on foreign energy sources from unstable countries and reduce regulatory barriers.

Source: The Contract From America, on Jul 8, 2010

NOTE: *In 2016, the phrase "all-of-the-above" has come to mean support of investing in alternative energy while simultaneously supporting nuclear power and more oil and gas drilling. The focus of an "all-of-the-above" stance is to decrease America's dependence on imported oil, by increasing domestic supplies of oil plus other energy sources, rather than a focus on replacing oil with renewable energy sources. Jeb's phrase "patriotic energy policy" (p. 175) implies the same focus on domestic sources.*

Jeb Bush on Renewable Energy

Replace crony capitalism with free-market strategy

Bush laid out ways conservatives can advance the "American idea" that the dinner's namesake advocated. Bush advocated free market principles, especially in energy policy. "We should let market forces, not crony capitalism, decide where to invest and how to incentivize citizens to conserve," Bush said, advocating approval of the Keystone XL pipeline, "rational" regulations on fracking, and opening federal lands to drilling. "A real energy strategy could add an additional 1% growth over the long haul."

Source: Tal Kopan on Politico.com, "Crony Capitalism" on Oct. 29, 2013

Set goal of 25% renewable energy by 2025

Bush endorsed a Congressional resolution that it is the goal of the United States that, not later than January 1, 2025, the agricultural, forestry, and working land of the US should provide from renewable resources not less than 25% of the total energy consumed and continue to produce safe, abundant, and affordable food, feed, and fiber. [Governors signed letters of endorsement at www.25x25.org, including Jeb Bush].

Rep. SALAZAR: "Our resolution establishes a national goal of producing 25% of America's energy from renewable sources—like solar, wind and biofuels—by 2025. The "25x'25" vision is widely endorsed, bold, and fully attainable. If implemented, it would dramatically improve our energy security, our economy, and our ability to protect the environment.

"I am pleased that the "25x'25" vision has been endorsed by 22 current and former governors. The Big Three automobile manufacturers—Ford, Chrysler, and General Motors—are all behind "25x'25" So are many agricultural organizations, environmental groups, scientists, and businesses. It is time for Congress to take a more active role in our clean energy future. Establishing a national goal—"25x'25" is the first step."

Source: 25x'25 Act (S.CON.RES.3 / H.CON.RES.25) on Jan. 17, 2007

Rand Paul on Government Reform

Audit federal agencies, to reform or eliminate them

Paul signed the *Contract From America* [which includes]:

- *Restore Fiscal Responsibility and Constitutionally Limited Government in Washington:*
- Create a Blue Ribbon taskforce that engages in a complete audit of federal agencies and programs, assessing their Constitutionality.
- *Stop the Pork:*
- Place a moratorium on all earmarks until the budget is balanced, and then require a 2/3 majority to pass any earmark.
- *Protect the Constitution:*
- Require each bill to identify the specific provision of the Constitution that gives Congress the power to do what the bill does.

Source: The Contract From America, on Jul 8, 2010

NOTE: *"Privatization" is a politicized word that means the same thing as term "out-sourcing" in the business world. The EPA, for example, is largely "privatized": most federal environmental work is implemented by private contractors selected through a competitive bidding process. The NIH, in another form of "privatization," provides grants for scientific research and development, also selected through a competitive application process. The EPA and NIH focus on enforcing regulations and overseeing contract and grant completion.*

Jeb Bush on Government Reform

Privatize & outsource government; fee holidays for contractors

Senate Bill 1016 is a broad piece of legislation dealing with the regulation of professions. It also implements a number of the Administration's priorities reflecting a smaller, more efficient government. Among these priorities, Senate Bill 1016 provides a "fee holiday" for 14 professions, ranging from electrical contractors to veterinarians to surveyors. Over the course of the next two years, the fee holidays will provide over $18 million in savings to these professions.

Senate Bill 1016 also encourages the privatization and outsourcing of certain governmental activities. It calls for the privatization of elevator inspections and contains provisions known collectively as the Management Privatization Act. These provisions will allow for the outsourcing of licensing and investigative functions of regulated professions.

Source: Approval notification on Senate Bill 1016, June 23, 2000

Mature society can empty government buildings of workers

Like other governmental conservatives, Governor Bush disliked and distrusted government and promoted the idea that smaller government—combined with more privatizing of governmental services—was more efficient government. He argued that "the most efficient, effective and dynamic government is one composed primarily of policymakers, procurement experts and contract managers." He expressed his general philosophy about government in his 2003 Inaugural Address when he stated that "There would be no greater tribute to our maturity as a society than if we make these [governmental] buildings around us empty of workers, monuments to a time when government played a larger role than it deserve or could adequately fill."

Source: Aggressive Conservatism in Florida, by Robert Crew, p. 30, Dec. 11, 2009

Rand Paul on Campaign Finance Reform

Federal contracts should include no-PAC clauses

I will propose that any federal contracts over a million dollars include a clause that precludes that entity from PAC contributions and lobbying.

Source: The Tea Party Goes to Washington, by Rand Paul, p.246, Feb 22, 2011

Lobbyists' sole goal is to rip you off

Last year, over 15,000 individuals worked for organizations whose sole goal was to rip you off. No, not the mafia or Goldman Sachs, but another distinctly criminal class—Washington lobbyists. In 2008, corporations and unions spent over $3 billion to bribe officials who claim to work for you.

Source: Senate campaign website, www.randpaul2010.com, "Issues," Jul 19, 2010

NOTE: 'PAC money' means donations to political action committees, which is used for issue ads which typically favor one candidate, but do not count in federal spending limits. 'soft money' means donations to the national party rather than to a particular candidate ($193 million in the 1998 election, for example). 'Hard money' is subject to less reform proposals—it means cash donations to a particular candidate, which must be fully reported to the FEC. Individuals may donate a maximum of $1000 to one candidate, but may donate any amount of soft money, and any amount to PACs. Candidates who voluntarily limit their campaign spending qualify for federal matching funds of about $100 million. Supporting campaign spending limits in 2016 implies opposing Citizens United or replacing McCain-Feingold.

Jeb Bush on Campaign Finance Reform

Complete transparency for campaigns & PAC donations

Florida is so flush with special-interest cash that our state is drowning in it. Even former Gov. Jeb Bush—a staunch defender of money in politics—believes reform is needed.

I asked the former governor about the current state of money in Florida politics. His response: "I am for complete transparency within 24 hours for all groups, committees, organizations, campaigns, PACs, etc." Right now, donations can remain secret for months.

Personally, I'd go further than Jeb Bush and crack down on these unlimited donations and secretive, under-regulated committees in general. But at a minimum, Bush is right that complete—and rapid—transparency is needed.

Source: Orlando Sentinel, "Megadonors taint Florida politics",
by Scott Maxwell, Aug. 18, 2012

No campaign spending limits; no public financing

Q: Do you support requiring full and timely disclosure of campaign finance information?

A: Yes.

Q: Do you support imposing spending limits on state level political campaigns?

A: No.

Q: Do you support partial funding from state taxes for state level political campaigns?

A: No.

Source: Florida Gubernatorial NPAT Test, Nov. 1, 1998

NOTE: *"Citizens United" refers to a 2010 Supreme Court case which allowed unlimited spending by "'super-PACs" on behalf of any candidate, as long as the TV ads are not coordinated with the campaign itself. Super-PACs dominate the spending in the 2012 presidential primaries and 2014 midterm elections, and will continue to do so in the 2016 elections.*

Rand Paul on Business Tax Reform

Cut corporate tax in half to create millions of jobs

With my five-year budget, millions of jobs would be created by cutting the corporate income tax in half, by creating a flat personal income tax of 17%, and by cutting the regulations that are strangling American businesses. The only stimulus ever proven to work is leaving more money in the hands of those who earned it!

Source: Tea Party Response to State of the Union Address, Feb. 12, 2013

NOTE: Democrats and liberals, in general (and President Obama in particular), want to increase corporate taxation by closing loopholes and removing tax breaks (not by increasing the corporate tax rate). Republicans and conservatives, in general, want to reduce the corporate tax rate, in some cases reducing it to zero.

The case for reducing the rate is that the US rate is among the highest in the world: at 35%, compared to 16% for Germany and Canada, and 2nd only to Japan's corporate rate. The case for removing loopholes is that the effective US rate is only about 25%, comparable to the average rate for the industrialized world, due to the numerous available deductions and tax breaks. Of the 500 major companies in the S&P 500, 115 paid a tax rate under 20% over the past five years, and 40 paid a tax rate under 10%. Pres. Obama's deficit-reduction committee recommends reducing the corporate tax rate to 23% while closing most loopholes. GOP candidates recommend reducing the corporate tax rate, in conjunction with a "tax holiday" for corporate repatriation.

Jeb Bush on Business Tax Reform

Remove Intangibles Tax on stocks, bonds & dividends

Over the course of his administration the Bush legislation produced $19.1 billion in tax cuts. The centerpiece of Bush's tax-reform effort was the abolition of the state's Intangible Personal Property Tax.

When Governor Bush came into office, Florida was one of only a handful of states that utilized some form of an intangibles tax. This tax was levied on stocks, bonds, mutual funds, money market funds, and other such investments. "By design, the tax is aimed at the state's wealthier residents" and in the absence of an income tax was initiated to derive at least some revenue from the personal income of wealthy citizens and corporations. While it was the most progressive of the taxes employed by the state, it was described by the governor as "evil and insidious," "counterproductive and unfair." Governor Bush worked to reduce it in every legislative session between 1999 and 2006, when it was finally abolished. Its elimination accounted for nearly 30% of the tax cuts he initiated.

Source: Aggressive Conservatism in Florida, by Robert Crew, p.102-3,
Dec. 11, 2009

Cutting "intangibles tax" helps "seniors and savers"

Saying that you're helping the rich doesn't play well, so Jeb and his people came up with a host of other reasons to eliminate the state's one tax on the rich: the tax's inefficiency; its alleged "unfairness."

Jeb knew it would be tough to create any public empathy for the actual "victims" of this tax, and so he and his people invented a new description for them: "seniors and savers." They produced statistics to show that a disproportionate number of people who paid this tax were elderly. And indeed, many of them probably were "savers."

Source: America's Next Bush, by S.V. Dáte, p.279-280, Feb. 15, 2007

Rand Paul on Inheritance Tax

Repeal tax hikes in capital gains and death tax

Paul signed the *Contract From America* [which includes]:

- **Stop the Tax Hikes:** Permanently repeal all tax hikes, including those to the income, capital gains, and death taxes, currently scheduled to begin in 2011.

- **Enact Fundamental Tax Reform:** Adopt a simple and fair single-rate tax system by scrapping the internal revenue code and replacing it with one that is no longer than 4,543 words—the length of the original Constitution.

- **Demand a Balanced Budget:** Begin the Constitutional amendment process to require a balanced budget with a two-thirds majority needed for any tax hike.

Source: The Contract From America, on Jul 8, 2010

NOTE: The 'Estate Tax' or 'Inheritance Tax' is called the 'death Tax' by its opponents, beginning in 2001 under President Bush. While polls indicate broad support for eliminating the estate tax, few Americans are directly affected by it. Opponents point out that some family businesses would have to sold to pay the estate tax. In 2001, 98% of descendants avoid taxes altogether because the first $675,000 of an estate was exempt from taxation. That exemption rose to $5 million in 2011-2012, with a one-year repeal in 2010, and is slated to return to $1 million in 2013. According to the Internal Revenue Service, about 3,000 estates are worth more than $5 million each and hence would be subject to the tax in 2011-2012.

The most popular sales tax on the Republican side is the 'FairTax,' which would replace the current progressive marginal rates with a single 'flat' rate (plans vary from 10% to 17%), applied after a deductible base. Flat Tax plans can achieve lower rates by removing the mortgage interest and charitable deductions. Jeb has mixed views on sales taxes; endorses repealing the estate tax; and has been silent so far on the FairTax.

Jeb Bush on Inheritance Tax

Supports estate tax repeal, but not at states' expense

Even as they deal with declining revenue growth from a softening economy, states are scrambling to plan for the potential loss of $50 billion to $100 billion over 10 years from the repeal of the federal estate tax enacted last month. The loss in revenue would come because states for 75 years have tied their own estate and inheritance taxes to the federal estate tax.

Governors are also chafing under a Congressional timetable that calls for the states to lose their tax revenues by 2005 while stretching the repeal of the federal estate tax more gradually over 10 years. Jeb Bush warned about anticipated revenue shortfalls [in Florida], including the expected loss of $210 million from the estate tax in the 2002-03 fiscal year. "While I support the eventual repeal of the estate tax," Mr. Bush, the president's brother, wrote, "shifting the burden merely allows Washington to spend more, while requiring us to spend less."

Source: Kevin Sack, NY Times, June 21, 2001

1987: supported sales service tax; 1998: opposed it

As Gov. Bob Martinez's Secretary of Commerce in 1987-88, perhaps Jeb's most memorable episode was his public support for the issue that proved to be Martinez' undoing: an expansion of the sales tax onto services, rather than just goods. Martinez originally endorsed the plan and then—under pressure from advertisers—called a special session for its repeal. The governor was never able to recover from this phenomenal flip-flop, and was easily defeated in 1990. In early 1987, Jeb came out solidly behind his boss: "If this is a way to broaden taxation and at the same time lower the rate, a lot of people would really go for it."

Even as he was publicly supporting the services tax, he had privately sent Martinez a letter telling him it was a bad idea. And in 1998, Jeb was able to produce the letter when his Democratic opponent started talking about the services tax and how Jeb had once supported it.

Source: America's Next Bush, by S.V. Dáte, p. 79-80, Feb. 15, 2007

Rand Paul on Tax Reform

Supports the Taxpayer Protection Pledge

Paul signed the Taxpayer Protection Pledge against raising taxes: [The ATR, Americans for Tax Reform, run by conservative lobbyist Grover Norquist, ask legislators to sign the Taxpayer Protection Pledge in each election cycle. Their self-description:] In the Taxpayer Protection Pledge, candidates and incumbents solemnly bind themselves to oppose any and all tax increases. Since its rollout in 1986, the pledge has become *de rigeur* for Republicans seeking office, and is a necessity for Democrats running in Republican districts. Today the Taxpayer Protection Pledge is offered to every candidate for state office and to all incumbents. More than 1,100 state officeholders, from state representative to governor, have signed the Pledge.

The Taxpayer Protection Pledge: "I pledge to the taxpayers of my district and to the American people that I will: ONE, oppose any and all efforts to increase the marginal income tax rate for individuals and business; and TWO, oppose any net reduction or elimination of deductions and credits, unless matched dollar for dollar by further reducing tax rates."

Source: Taxpayer Protection Pledge on Jan 1, 2012

Stand firm and say NO to any MORE tax hikes!

This year, they say they will have a budget, but after just recently imposing hundreds of billions in new taxes, they now say they will include more tax hikes in their budget. We must stand firm. We must say NO to any MORE tax hikes!

Only through lower taxes, less regulation and more freedom will the economy begin to grow again. Our party is the party of growth, jobs and prosperity, and we will boldly lead on these issues.

Source: Tea Party Response to State of the Union Address, Feb. 12, 2013

Jeb Bush on Tax Reform

Compromise on taxes ok, as part of a spending cut package

Q: You have taken some heat for your suggestion that you might be willing to accept higher taxes as part of a grand bargain, if you also got serious spending cuts, and you also gotten some entitlement reform. Anti-tax advocate Grover Norquist said: "People are looking for someone who's tough and you are saying, 'I'll fold.'"

BUSH: What we ought to be focused on in Washington is to build consensus on the things where there's an agreement. Maybe that would be on creating sustained economic growth which creates more revenue than any tax increase. But I don't think that you should automatically say, "No. Heck, no." We have to find in a divided country ways to forge compromise. [Reagan] did exactly that, he forged consensus, he compromised, he didn't violate his principles. So, the idea that you have to have this doctrinaire view [like Grover Norquist's "No taxes" pledge], but you're not necessarily going to be able to solve these pressing problems that we have.

Source: Fox News Sunday interview, March 10, 2013

No pledge on taxes; trade-offs on taxes means leadership

Perhaps the greatest sin in the modern conservative movement is George H. W. Bush's 1990 budget deal where he traded tax increases for budget savings. Jeb Bush has cited his father's compromise as the epitome of presidential leadership.

In his positions on fiscal policy, Jeb Bush has given comfort to the suspicious. When asked about the hypothetical trade-off posited during a 2012 GOP debate, where no GOP candidate would accept a dollar of tax increases in exchange for 10 dollars in spending reductions, Jeb Bush took a different view. "If you could bring to me a majority of people to say that we're going to have $10 in spending cuts for $1 of revenue enhancement—put me in, coach," he said at the time.

Source: John Dickerson on Slate.com, "Hard on the GOP," March 31, 2014

Rand Paul vs. Jeb Bush
on Entitlement Issues

Entitlement issues focus on the recession recovery and all forms of entitlements. The term "entitlements" implies that these programs are guaranteed and immutable, but in reality, they are subject to Congressional changes just like any other law. The duration of unemployment benefits, for example, has been changed regularly since the Great Recession began. And ObamaCare, the newest (and potentially largest) entitlement, can and likely will be changed by new laws as the program comes into full force. Even Social Security, once considered the "third rail" of politics because even *discussing* changing the program entailed political suicide, has been open to modification since George W. Bush publicly discussed it as president. This chapter includes the following sections:

- *Health Care (pp. 76-83):* including federal healthcare and ObamaCare issues; plus Medicare/Medicaid and state issues. The two candidates both oppose ObamaCare, but Jeb is not a hard-core repealist on the subject: he says we should let ObamaCare fail on its own. Rand Paul, as a formerly practicing M.D., opposes ObamaCare from a personal perspective as well as libertarian perspective. The same applies to Medicare/Medicaid: Rand opposes Medicare choice; Jeb would convert Medicaid to a voucher system, and other changes, but again keeping the core program in place. A key question for Jeb in 2015 is whether his anti-ObamaCare stance is strong enough, or if Rand Paul and other Tea Party opponents will challenge him on this issue in the primary (since "repealing and replacing" ObamaCare is a core tenet of the Tea Party, with which Jeb does not agree).

- *Jobs (pp. 84-89):* including unemployment and union issues. Depending on the state of the Great Recession, federal job assistance might become an issue in 2016 (such as extending unemployment insurance, or jobs-creation programs). If the unemployment rate continues slowly falling as it did throughout 2014, there will not be any jobs-based issues in 2016 except the usual ongoing issues (unions and affirmative action). Jeb would restrict unions and cut taxes instead of extending unemployment compensation; Rand agrees with those policies but for different underlying reasons. Rand is a hard-core activist against affirmative action issues; Jeb is moderately anti-affirmative action.

- *Education (pp. 90-99):* This is a core issue for Jeb, and Rand has voted on all of those issues, so we include a lot of aspects. Jeb agrees with the national standards of Common Core; this issue invites opposition from Rand Paul and other Tea Party primary opponent, since opposing Common Core is a hot issue within the Tea Party and libertarians. Jeb, like his brother George, has pushed hard for school choice (which Rand also supports); that is the goal of those who would abolish Common Core, so Jeb might blunt the GOP primary attack by supporting both issues. Rand most strongly disagrees with Jeb on "No Child Left Behind," which Jeb supports (his brother George initiated it while President).

- *Social Security (pp. 100-101):* including the current Trust Fund and changes for the future. Jeb supported privatization of many state programs while Governor of Florida, but has not applied that philosophy to Social Security. Rand supports raising the Social Security retirement age, which means tweaking the system without calling for privatization. Neither has made this issue a focus; perhaps other primary opponents will.

- *Welfare & Poverty (pp. 102-105):* including homelessness, welfare payments, and other poverty programs. Jeb and Rand agree on most aspects of this issue: both oppose welfare on moral grounds, and both support collaborating with faith-based organizations (initiated by Pres. George W. Bush in the 2000s). More on religion in our Social Issues chapter (p. 106ff)

Rand Paul on Entitlement Issues

Jeb Bush on Entitlement Issues

Rand Paul on ObamaCare

Compassion cannot be delivered in the form of coercion

It is a noble aspiration and a moral obligation to make sure our fellow man is provided for, that medical treatment is made available to all. But compassion cannot be delivered in the form of coercion.

President Obama's fundamental promise that if you like your doctor you can keep them—was a lie. ObamaCare, at its core, takes away a patient's right to choose. Under ObamaCare, patients are prohibited from choosing their doctor or their insurance. Today, more Americans may have medical insurance, but Americans are now paying more money for worse care.

The relationship between doctor and patient is withering. Doctors are fleeing the profession they love. Hospitals are straining, closing, or refusing to accept ObamaCare policies. Everyone knows our health care system needed reforming, but it was the wrong prescription to choose more government instead of more consumer choice and competition. How should we fix our healthcare system? Let's try freedom again. It worked for over 200 years!

Source: Tea Party response to the State of the Union, Jan. 20, 2015

ObamaCare cuts hundreds of choices down to just four

Q: One of the success stories of ObamaCare is in your own state: 26,000 people have signed up on the Kentucky web site. Can ObamaCare can be a success?

PAUL: Nearly 90% of them are signing up for Medicaid, free health insurance from the government. My concern is not that we shouldn't help people. I do want to help these people to get insurance. But there is going to be a cost. So I see the positive, but I also see the negative. And the real problem is we're driving everyone out of the individual market. Where there were once hundreds of plans that you could choose from, there's now four government-mandated plans. If your insurance is not as good as them, or even if it's too good, you can't buy it.

Source: ABC This Week interview: Nov 3, 2013

Jeb Bush on ObamaCare

ObamaCare is flawed to its core

Jeb Bush said that President Barack Obama's health care law "is flawed to its core" and will be a "big problem" for Democrats heading into the 2014 elections. "I don't think it will work," Bush said of ObamaCare. Bush added, "If the objective is, don't worry about the budget, we'll just finance it the same way we're financing our deficits right now, build a bigger debt, you could see this thing surviving," he said. "But it will have failed what the promises were. It will have failed the American people. And I don't think it will bend the cost curve."

Bush has emerged over the years as a strong proponent of what he calls "consumer-directed health care." He noted that he underwent knee surgery a month ago and forced himself into the conversation on billing. "The whole experience is opaque," he said. "It's like smoke comes up, you don't know what's really happening, the third party pays."

Source: Bill Glauber of the Milwaukee Journal Sentinel on Nov. 4, 2013

Let ObamaCare fail due to its own dysfunction

Q: This government shutdown started with House Republicans saying that they wanted to gut ObamaCare and they were willing to not fund the government until that happened. Your thoughts?

BUSH: Tactically it was a mistake to focus on something that couldn't be achieved. I would argue that allowing ObamaCare to be implemented, two things would happen. One, it would be so dysfunctional if it was implemented faithfully. Or it couldn't be implemented because the government is not capable of doing it. It looks like that, the latter rather than the former, may be happening. I think the best way to repeal ObamaCare is to have an alternative. We could do this in a much lower cost with improved quality based on free market principles. And show how ObamaCare, flawed to its core, doesn't work. It might actually be a politically better approach to see the massive dysfunction.

Source: ABC This Week interview, Oct. 20, 2013

Rand Paul on Medicare/Medicaid

Voted NO on the Ryan Budget: against Medicare choice

Proponent's Arguments for voting YES: [Sen. Ayotte, R-NH]: We have 3 choices when it comes to addressing rising health care costs in Medicare. We can do nothing & watch the program go bankrupt in 2024. We can go forward with the President's proposal to ration care through an unelected board of 15 bureaucrats. Or we can show real leadership & strengthen the program to make it solvent for current beneficiaries, and allow future beneficiaries to make choices.

Opponent's Arguments for voting NO: [Sen. Merkley, D-OR]: The Republicans chose to end Medicare as we know it. The Republican plan reopens the doughnut hole. That is the hole into which seniors fall when, after they have some assistance with the first drugs they need, they get no assistance until they reach a catastrophic level. It is in that hole that seniors have had their finances devastated. We fixed it. Republicans want to unfix it and throw seniors back into the abyss. Then, instead of guaranteeing Medicare coverage for a fixed set of benefits for every senior—as Medicare does now—the Republican plan gives seniors a coupon and says: Good luck. Go buy your insurance. If the insurance goes up, too bad.

Senator Rand Paul voted NO. Status: Failed 40-57

Reference: Ryan Budget Plan; Bill SCR21; vote #77 on May 25, 2011

NOTE: *Medicaid Expansion: Under ObamaCare, the limit for qualifying for Medicaid is raised from 130% to 133% of the poverty line, with subsidies for families earning up to 150% of the poverty line. As of September 2014, 27 states have adopted the Medicaid expansion (including Rand Paul's Kentucky, but not including Jeb Bush's Florida).*

For states that do expand Medicaid, the federal government pays for 100% of the expansion through 2016, and the subsidy tapers to 90% by 2020. Several opposing states argue that their 10% responsibility of funding the expansion will be too much for their states' budgets.

Jeb Bush on Medicare/Medicaid

Move Medicaid from "defined benefit" to defined contribution

Bush proposed an overhaul of Medicaid that reflected another major philosophical shift in the state's program, moving it from a "defined benefit" to a "defined contribution" basis. The proposal had two significant features. The first was acceptance of a lump sum of money from the federal government to fund the state's program in exchange for flexibility to determine eligibility and benefits levels. The state took on the responsibility for meeting the health-care needs of its residents regardless of whether the costs to do so exceeded the amount negotiated between Tallahassee and Washington. If costs exceeded negotiated levels, Florida would be able to use the flexibility granted by the federal government to impose benefit restrictions and cap program enrollment in order to contain costs. This provision was designed to permit the state to more accurately predict and control its costs.

The second major change was to provide each person with a risk-adjusted allotment of funds (a voucher which the state called a premium) with which to purchase health care. Using this voucher, enrollees were required to purchase a health-care plan from a participating managed-care organization. The benefit package offered had to be actuarially equivalent to the existing Medicaid benefit.

To entice companies to insure some of Florida's sickest and poorest citizens, the state proposed to cap Medicaid benefits, and set a ceiling on spending for each recipient. Managed-care companies and other health-care networks would design alternative health plans that Medicaid patients would use. Beyond that, different managed-care networks could attract patients by offering additional services. However, patients would have a choice only among managed-care plans and no longer have access to traditional fee-for-service health care.

Source: Aggressive Conservatism in Florida, by Robert Crew, p. 38, Dec. 11, 2009

Rand Paul on Mental Health

No mandatory mental health screening in schools

S.1800: Parental Consent Act: Sponsor: Sen Rand Paul [KY]

- Prohibits federal funds from being used to implement any universal or mandatory mental health or socioemotional screening program.

- Prohibits federal education funds to any local educational agency that uses the refusal to provide consent to mental health screening as the basis of a charge of child abuse or neglect.

- Defines a screening program as any mental health screening in which an individual is automatically screened without regard to whether there was a prior indication of a need.

Rep. Ron Paul remarks: Universal or mandatory mental-health screening threatens to undermine parents' right to raise their children as the parents see fit. Forced mental-health screening could lead to more children being improperly placed on psychotropic drugs, or stigmatized as "mentally ill" because they adhere to traditional values. Congress has a responsibility to the nation's parents & children to stop this from happening. We owe it to older adults in this country to do all that we can to ensure that high quality mental health care is both available and accessible. This legislation takes an important step in that direction.

LEGISLATIVE OUTCOME: Referred to Senate Committee on Health, Education, Labor, and Pensions; never came to a vote.

Source: Library of Congress, S.1800, Parental Consent Act, Nov. 3, 2011

Jeb Bush on Mental Health

Slashed every request for adult mental health

Bush's lowest spending priorities were for Florida's agencies dealing with its most vulnerable citizens.

One embarrassing consequence of his lack of attention to social services agencies emerged in the days just before Bush left office when his secretary of the Department of Children and Families was fined and threatened with jail time for failure to provide enough beds to treat county jail inmates with severe mental illness. Records from the department showed that it had called repeatedly for funds for adult health and that Bush had slashed every request—in 1 year by 93% (Hunt, 2006; Rushing, 2006). To avoid court sanctions, the governor was forced to ask the Legislative Budget Commissions, an organization that authorizes appropriations when the legislature itself is not in session, for an additional $16.6 million for hundreds of new beds for these individuals.

*Source: Aggressive Conservatism in Florida, by Robert Crew, p.107,
Dec. 11, 2009*

NOTE: *ObamaCare suggested some mental health coverage but the details are left to each state. Mental health is one of ObamaCare's "10 Essential Health Benefits." This is an example of healthcare issues that were not fully worked out under ObamaCare, and will be left to the 2016 election to decide.*

Rand Paul on Medical Malpractice

Supports tort reform & free-market principles

As a doctor, I have had firsthand experience with the vast problems facing health care in the United States. Like other areas of the economy in which the federal government wields its heavy hand, health care is over-regulated and in need of serious market reforms. Government interventions in health care have driven up the cost of coverage. I have long supported making all medical expenses tax deductible, allowing insurance to be bought across state lines, tort reform (state-level), and empowering all citizens to save for health expenses by removing the high-deductible insurance policy requirement to access to Health Savings Accounts.

More freedom to choose and innovate will make sure our health care system remains the best in the world. As your Senator, I am working to ensure that real free market principles are applied to the American health care system so that it is responsive to patients, families, and doctors rather than government bureaucracy.

Source: Official Senate website, www.paul.senate.gov, Jan. 15, 2015

Jeb Bush on Medical Malpractice

Compromised on limiting medical malpractice awards

Jeb stood in the Capitol rotunda, a pained smile on his face, explaining how he was glad that he and lawmakers were able to come to a reasonable compromise on his plan to limit pain and suffering jury awards to medical malpractice victims.

Jeb was saying this, but it was obvious that he wasn't enjoying it, probably because everyone knew it wasn't true. The "compromise" was hardly that—more like a near-total capitulation on Jeb's part. Behind him, state senators stood in the familiar semicircle of solidarity, but they were scarcely able to contain their glee.

Then, after hands were shaken and the senators had withdrawn to their private office, there were laughs and high fives all around. "This is probably the first time he's ever been spanked," crowed one. Said another: "I don't want to gloat. Well, yes I do."

Source: America's Next Bush, by S.V. Dáte, p.129, Feb. 15, 2007

NOTE: *"Tort Reform" refers to changing the rules about civil litigation, typically to cap damage awards. In a political context, it usually applies to medical malpractice lawsuits, but in a legal context, it also applies to personal injury and product liability lawsuits. The term "tort" means "at fault;" when a doctor is found at fault, a jury can currently award unlimited damages. Awards in the millions of dollars put upward pressure on malpractice insurance rates; hence many conservatives favor tort reform as a means to reduce healthcare costs. Proposed solutions include capping lawsuit compensation or restricting "frivolous lawsuits." Trial lawyers—the recipients of legal fees from tort awards—heavily favor Democratic candidates, so Republicans would like to limit their legal fees.*

Rand Paul on Union Policy

National Right-to-Work Act: no forced unionization

Sen. Paul introduced his National Right-to-Work Act, S.204, subtitled "A bill to preserve and protect the free choice of individual employees to form, join, or assist labor organizations, or to refrain from such activities."

Indiana has joined the growing list of right to work (RTW) states, followed by heavily-unionized Michigan. That means that forced unionism is still legal in 26 states, but that number is dwindling.

RTW laws are still government intervention into what used to be private matters between employers and employees, but they lift the most onerous parts of labor union agreements which demand either the complete exclusion of non-union workers from being employed by a union shop or requiring any non-union workers to support the union with their dues anyway.

In his announcement, Paul stated: "Every American worker deserves the right to freedom of association—and I am concerned that the 26 states that allow forced union membership and dues infringes on these workers' rights."

Source: The New American, Feb. 13, 2013

NOTE: *"Right-to-Work" refers to a state law against requiring union membership. The opposite is a "union shop" (or "closed shop"), where employees are required to pay union dues as a condition for working. 22 states are "right-to-work" states (mostly in the South and West) and 28 are not. A "national right-to-work law" would abolish union shops, and convert them all to "open shops," where employees may join the union voluntarily but are not required.*

Jeb Bush on Union Policy

School choice is about unions versus kids

There are many people who say they support strong schools but draw the line at school choice. "Sorry, kid. Giving you equal opportunity would be too risky. And it will upset powerful political forces that we need to win elections."

I have a simple message for these masters of delay and deferral: Choose. You can either help the politically powerful unions. Or you can help the kids. Now, I know it's hard to take on the unions. They fund campaigns. But you and I know who deserves a choice.

Source: Republican National Convention speech, Aug. 29, 2012

Employ American Workers Act led to lost ideas & lost jobs

Buried inside [the 2009 stimulus] was a union-backed provision called the Employ American Workers Act, which restricted H-1B visas for any company that received federal recovery assistance. "Within days of the president signing it into law," recounts a professor at the Tuck School of Business at Dartmouth College, "a number of US banks reneged on job offers extended months earlier to foreign-born MBA students." The net result, says Slaughter: "Lost ideas. Lost jobs. Lost taxes."

Source: Immigration Wars, by Jeb Bush, p. 93, March 5, 2013

NOTE: Gov. Scott Walker (R-WI) pushed a "union-busting" bill in early 2011, restricting collective bargaining rights of all public employees, including teachers. The bill passed, but large-scale protests led to a recall election in 2012. Gov. Walker survived the recall, and got re-elected in 2014. In July 2014, the Wisconsin Supreme Court upheld the law. Jeb's reference to "unions versus kids" means he takes Gov. Walker's side.

Rand Paul on Employment Policy

Extending unemployment benefits does disservice to workers

Q: Do you support extending unemployment benefits, or would you let 1.3 million Americans lose those benefits?

PAUL: I do support unemployment benefits for the 26 weeks that they're paid for. If you extend it beyond that, you do a disservice to these workers. There was a study that came out a few months ago, and it said, if you have a worker that's been unemployed for 4 weeks and on unemployment insurance and one that's on 99 weeks, which would you hire? Every employer, nearly 100%, said they will always hire the person who's been out of work 4 weeks. When you allow people to be on unemployment insurance for 99 weeks, you're causing them to become part of this perpetual unemployed group in our economy. And while it seems good, it actually does a disservice to the people you're trying to help.

Source: Fox News Sunday interview, Dec. 8, 2013

Unemployment insurance ok if fully paid for & short-term

Q: What about extending benefits to the unemployed? President Obama in his weekly address said it's cruel to deny those benefits.

PAUL: Well, I think what's really cruel is to have an economy that doesn't have jobs in it. So we have to talk about what policy creates jobs. With regard to unemployment insurance, I'm not opposed to unemployment insurance, I am opposed to having it without paying for it. I think it's wrong to borrow money from China or simply to print up money for it. But I'm not against having unemployment insurance. I do think, though, that the longer you have it, that it provides some disincentive to work, and that there are many studies that indicate this.

Q: But if this extension is paid for, you can support it

PAUL: Well, what I have always said is that it needs to be paid for, but we also need to do something for long-term unemployed people, and that is, we need to create something new that creates jobs.

Source: ABC This Week interview, Jan. 11, 2014

Jeb Bush on Employment Policy

Cutting taxes on job creators benefits everyone

The biggest tax cut of Jeb's time in office, the intangibles tax, had diminished the state treasury by $1 billion a year. An analysis of that policy starts with two fundamental questions.

1. Given Florida's poor rankings in various quality-of-life measures, were large tax cuts appropriate public policy?
2. Once you have decided that tax cuts were appropriate, was the intangibles tax the most appropriate one to cut?

On the first question, Jeb is part of the wing of the Republican Party that believes as a fundamental truth that taxes are too high. Period. The second question: if you cut taxes on the rich, everyone benefits. There, in a nutshell, is the Bush Family Economic Theory, boiled down to nine words. The emphasis is not to cut taxes for everybody—[but to] cut proportionately more for the wealthy—or, in Bush parlance, the investor class, the risk takers, the job creators.

Source: America's Next Bush, by S.V. Dáte, p.277-278, Feb. 15, 2007

Job growth during Bush terms, but very low wage jobs

In his 2006-2007 Budget Message he cited the lowest unemployment rate in the nation and an "unprecedented" job creation rate. While there was job growth during the Bush term of office it was smaller than in any gubernatorial administration since 1978. In addition, much of the job growth was the product of a growing population rather than the tax cuts the governor generated.

Most of the jobs created during the Bush administration were in the low-paying sectors of the economy. The state's 2004 median hourly wage ($13.10 per hour) was below the national average and the state had an unusually high percentage of very low-wage workers who earned wages at or below the federal minimum wage.

Source: Aggressive Conservatism in Florida, by Robert Crew, p.109-10, Dec. 11, 2009

Rand Paul on Affirmative Action

Women won the "war on women": they're no longer downtrodden

Q: What about the "war for women"?

PAUL: Well, you know, I think we have a lot of debates in Washington that get dumbed down. This whole sort of war on women thing, I'm scratching my head because if there was a war on women, I think they won. You know, the women in my family are incredibly successful. I have a niece at Cornell vet school, and 85% of the young people there are women. In law school, 60% are women; in med school, 55%. You know, I don't see so much that women are downtrodden; I see women rising up and doing great things. And, in fact, I worry about our young men sometimes because I think the women really are out-competing the men in our world. I think the facts show that women are doing very well, have come a long way. So I don't really see this, that there's some sort of war that's, you know, keeping women down.

Source: Meet the Press 2014 interview, Jan. 26, 2014

Illegal to impose racial segregation in the private sector

In two broadcast interviews, Paul said that the federal government may have overstepped its role by making it illegal to impose racial segregation in the private sector. Asked if he thought a private business had the right to say it would not serve black people, he said: "I don't want to be associated with those people, but I also don't want to limit their speech in any way in the sense that we tolerate boorish and uncivilised behaviour because that's one of the things freedom requires."

Since the furore, Paul has released a statement indicating that he would have voted for the Civil Rights Act of 1964 de-segregation bill, a position he declined to take a day earlier: "I support the Civil Rights Act because I overwhelmingly agree with the intent of the legislation, which was to stop discrimination in the public sphere and halt the abhorrent practice of segregation," he said.

Source: London Sunday Times, "US and the Americas," May 21, 2010

Jeb Bush on Affirmative Action

One Florida: equal minority contracts and admissions

The One Florida initiative was actually designed to maintain the status quo—to admit just as many black and Hispanic students to Florida universities and award just as many contracts to black and Hispanic businesses as was possible under affirmative action, except to do this without specifically using race. The college admissions, for example, would be done using a "Talented 20" scheme, in which students in the top 5th of any high school class would be guaranteed entrance to a public university, regardless of their actual grade point average or SAT scores. The net result was to be the same. Students in predominantly minority high schools who scored at the top of their class would have a huge leg up over white students in suburban schools.

This was a program that, had Jeb used some savvy in rolling it out, blacks and Hispanics could easily have embraced. Jeb's problem, as was typical, was that he reached out for their support only when it came time to roll out the proposal.

Source: America's Next Bush, by S.V. Dáte, p.187-188, Feb. 15, 2007

Insisted on more racial and gender diversity in trial judges

Florida's nominating commissions recommend candidates for the Florida Supreme Court, the district courts of appeal, and all midterm vacancies in the circuit and county courts. Since 2001, the governor has appointed not just three but all nine members of each commission. One way in which Governor Jeb Bush used his vastly increased influence was to insist on more racial and gender diversity on the trial bench. But he was criticized for making the process much more partisan, and for appointing several conspicuously ideological attorneys and politicians to the district courts of appeal.

Source: A Most Disorderly Court: Scandal and Reform in the Florida Judiciary, p. 162, by Martin Dyckman, March 30, 2008

Rand Paul on College Policy

Federal student loans are ok, if within spending limits

During the Q&A session after Sen. Paul's speech at Howard University, one student explained that he was not a fan of his view of government: "You say you want to provide a government that leaves us alone; quite frankly, I don't want that," the student said. "I want a government that is going to help me."

The student insisted that he wanted assistance for his college education and asked if Rand Paul supported a culture change within the nation. Paul responded that he believed that government should allow people to believe whatever they wanted, and clarified that he didn't believe in the absence of government.

The Kentucky Republican added that he supported the idea of student loans from the government but added that the federal government shouldn't be allowed to spend more money than it takes in: "I think 'leave me alone' is a good mantra for government because government has to be involved in certain things but there are many things that we can leave government out of," Paul concluded.

Source: Washington Examiner, April 10, 2013

NOTE: *President Obama in his 2015 State of the Union speech called for the American College Promise: that community college should be free for all students for two years (in other words, extending free high school two more years). Obama proposes spending $60 billion to full-time non-wealthy non-failing students, in states that opt-in to the program.*

Jeb Bush on College Policy

Guarantee college admission for top 20% of high school grads

After discussions failed to convince him to delay his initiative until 2002, Bush stepped in with an executive order banning racial and gender preferences in university admissions and state contracting. Called "One Florida" the governor's program guaranteed college admissions to the top 20% of each high school graduating class, provided that students had taken college preparatory classes. It also required agencies of Florida state government to make special efforts to reach out to minority contractors and to increase state business with such companies without the use of set-asides and price preferences.

Source: Aggressive Conservatism in Florida, by Robert Crew, p. 91, Dec. 11, 2009

Replaced college affirmative action with "One Florida" initiative

An ardent proponent of privatization, Bush helped eliminate nearly 14,000 jobs, and by executive order he replaced affirmative action in university admissions and state contracting with his own "One Florida" initiative, a move that generated lasting ill will with many in the African American community.

Bush was alternately dubbed the "best governor in America" by admirers and "King Jeb" by detractors, but few would dispute that [Bush will] "go down as one of Florida's most consequential governors."

Source: The Rise of Marco Rubio, by Manuel Rogi-Franzia, p.132, June 19, 2012

Rand Paul on Common Core

Block funding for Common Core; it's too heavy-handed

Letter to Tom Harkin, Chairman and Jerry Moran, Ranking Member of Subcommittee on Labor Health and Human Services, and Education, from Rand Paul and 14 additional Senators:

While the Common Core State Standards Initiative was initially billed as a voluntary effort between states, federal incentives have clouded the picture. The selection criteria designed by the U.S. Department of Education for the Race to the Top Program provided that for a state to have a reasonable chance to compete for funding, it must adopt a "common set of K-12 standards" matching the description of the Common Core. This heavy-handed push to get states to adopt the Common Core State Standards in such a short timeframe preempted an important public debate about the standards, which is now happening after the fact at the state level throughout the country.

Source: Letter from 15 Senators, April 4, 2014

NOTE: *The Common Core State Standards Initiative, begun in 2009, has been adopted fully by 32 states and partially adopted by 13 others. The Obama administration provided competitive 'Race to the Top' grants as an incentive for states to adopt the Common Core. The Common Core defines standards for math and English, with standards to come in the future for science and social studies. Because the standards are copyrighted, critics consider them to be a 'one-size-fits-all' model, and a step towards nationalizing America's schools.*

Jeb Bush on Common Core

Common Core lets 1,000 different curriculum flowers bloom

Q: How important is it to have national standards?

BUSH: I think higher standards is really the element of this that's most important. So if you dumb down the standards, everybody feels good. Little Johnny's going to get a piece of paper that says he's graduated from high school. But this massive remediation that's necessary to access higher education is evidence that we're not benchmarking ourselves to college readiness. So higher standards matter. The commonality of them—in this case 45 states—voluntarily creating them.

Q: The Common Core?

BUSH: The Common Core standards in language arts and math is important because curriculum is developed in this kind of system where there's common expectations. You'll have one thousand different flowers blooming as it relates to curriculum. It won't be homogenized, it will be diverse and alive which is what we need.

Q: But a lot of conservatives, certainly Tea Party movement, are very suspicious of this process. Standards means testing; you hear a common complaint, "We test too much."

BUSH: I think we do test too much. You could have fewer tests and achieve the desired results of transparency and accountability.

Source: ABC This Week interview, Oct. 20, 2013

1994: cut Department of Education from 2,000 to 50 staff

The cornerstone of Bush's 1994 campaign was a sweeping set of conservative proposals that, if enacted, would have made Florida a virtual laboratory for far-right policy: "I would abolish the Department of Education as it now exists, reducing the 2,000 person bureaucracy to about 50 to administer federal education funding and maintain minimum academic standards in Florida's schools," Bush told the Orlando Sentinel in a November 1994 interview.

Source: New York Times interview, "Evolving Views," Jan. 11, 2015

Rand Paul on No Child Left Behind

No Child Left Behind is federal takeover of schools

Sen. Rand Paul, in response to the announcement that President Barack Obama granted 10 states, including Kentucky, waivers for No Child Left Behind, released the following statement: "I applaud the President's decision to grant No Child Left Behind waivers to Kentucky and several other states," Sen. Paul said. "The implementation of this federal government takeover of our education system has hurt not helped parents, teachers, administrators, and most importantly, students.

"This waiver decision only serves to highlight the inherent problems with the federal takeover of education, and should remind us all that the best policy would be full repeal, with education decisions going back to the local governments, school administrators and parents. I am hopeful this decision also indicated President Obama has finally realized states would like relief from the burdensome mandates placed on them by the federal government," Sen. Paul concluded.

Source: Official Senate website www.paul.senate.gov, Feb. 10, 2012

NOTE: *No Child Left Behind (NCLB) is the 2001 bipartisan law intended to improve K-12 schools, under the theory of standards-based education reform. States are required to establish standardized testing, so that all high school graduates meet the test criteria. States are also required to give options (school choice) to students who attend schools that fail to meet NCLB's Adequate Yearly Progress (AYP).*

The controversy over NCLB currently focuses on funding: Opponents of NCLB argue that states are provided inadequate federal funding for implementation of NCLB, and that therefore NCLB represents an "unfunded mandate" on states. Proponents of NCLB argue that the law provides accountability for schools; fights against incompetent teachers; and provides alternatives to failing schools. Progress is measured in the federal National Assessment of Educational Progress (NAEP), commonly knows as the "Nation's Report Card."

Jeb Bush on No Child Left Behind

No Child Left Behind got states to start reforms

Q: "No Child Left Behind" was one of the great bipartisan achievements that your brother had. What's its legacy?

BUSH: I think "No Child Left Behind" pushed states that refused to begin the process of reform into the arena. So now every state is on the journey. Some really slow and some far more advanced. But ultimately this is a state-driven kind of enterprise. But the jump start for a lot of states that refused to use accountability and testing and a focus on early literacy and all the things that began with "No Child Left Behind" wouldn't have happened. So I think it served a useful purpose.

Q: How bad is the current system?

BUSH: If you measure it by outcomes, [only] 25% of kids pass all of the four segments of the ACT test which means that they're college-ready or career-ready. And about 20% don't graduate at all. That's failure.

Source: ABC This Week interview, Oct. 20, 2013

Florida Formula: schools graded A-to-F; extra funding for A

Bush's "Florida formula" rests on the principles of increasing accountability and expanding parental choice. Among its tenets:

- Grade schools on an A-to-F scale, based mostly on student scores and growth on standardized tests. Give students in poorly ranked schools vouchers to attend private and religious schools.

- Hold back 8-year-olds who can't pass a state reading test rather than promote them to fourth grade.

- Expand access to online classes and charter schools, which are publicly funded but privately managed.

Source: Stephanie Simon on Reuters, "Bush Foundation," Nov. 30, 2012

Rand Paul on Charter Schools

Charters & flexibility instead of federal one-size-fits-all

I believe in more local control over education, where states, localities, and parents can play a much more significant role in their children's schooling. The federal government has disregarded parental rights, and left kids with an unsatisfactory education. Innovation in education will never come from an overgrown federal bureaucracy, mandating standards and discounting local input.

I support reduced taxes and increased flexibility so families can choose the most effective educational institution for their child, whether it be public, private, charter, homeschool or online. I also seek to prevent the Department of Education from regulating private and homeschooling options.

I recognize the great potential of local schools and parents who are allowed the freedom to manage their own children's educational needs, according to the community they live in, as opposed to a one-size-fits-all federal government approach that has been proven to not work for most kids.

Source: Official Senate website www.paul.senate.gov, Jan. 15, 2015

NOTE: *'Charter schools' are publicly-funded and publicly-controlled schools which are privately run. They are usually required to adhere to fewer district rules than regular public schools. The first charter schools started in Minnesota in 1991.*

By 2011, there were 5,600 public charter schools enrolling more than two million students nationwide. More than 400,000 students remain on wait lists to attend charter schools. Over 500 new public charter schools opened their doors in the 2011-12 school year, an estimated increase of 200,000 students.

Jeb Bush on Charter Schools

800,000 FL parents selected schools, not district zoning

Starting in 1999, Florida embarked upon a series of reforms designed to improve public schools and broaden educational choices.

All parents should be empowered to choose the best schools for their children, and in Florida school choice is widespread. Last year in Florida, nearly 800,000 students attended schools selected by their parents, not by district zoning laws. More than 200,000 students attend public charter schools. About 25,000 special-needs children attend private schools using scholarships. Almost 50,000 students from low-income families receive scholarships funded by tax credits to attend the schools that best fit them.

Source: Immigration Wars, by Jeb Bush, p.184-185, March 5, 2013

NOTE: 'School Choice' generally refers to a school district allowing parents to decide which school within the district to send their kids to. The political issue is whether to allow the choice to include private schools, parochial schools, and home schooling at taxpayer expense. Taxpayer funding of parochial schools potentially violates the Constitutional separation of church and state. Taxpayer funding of private schools is controversial because it subsidizes parents who are currently paying for private schools themselves, and are usually more wealthy than the average public school family.

Rand Paul on School Vouchers

Allow school choice for everyone, white, brown, or black

For those striving to climb the ladder of success we must fix our schools. America's educational system is leaving behind anyone who starts with disadvantages. We have cut classroom size in half and tripled spending on education and still we lag behind much of the world.

A great education needs to be available for everyone, whether you live on Country Club Lane or in government housing. This will only happen when we allow school choice for everyone, rich or poor, white, brown, or black. Let the taxes you pay for education follow each and every student to the school of your choice.

Competition has made America the richest nation in history. Competition can make our educational system the envy of the world. The status quo traps poor children in a crumbling system of hopelessness. When every child can, like the President's kids, go to the school of their choice, then will the dreams of our children come true!

Source: Tea Party Response to State of the Union Address, Feb. 12, 2013

Support homeschooling and parental responsibility

Rand proposes to restore the parental right to be responsible in educating children. He supports reduced taxes so that parents can allocate more of their own funds to homeschooling, if they so desire.

Source: Senate campaign website, www.randpaul2010.com, "Issues," Jul 19, 2010

Jeb Bush on School Vouchers

Education savings accounts: Fund students instead of schools

The best way for education policy to catch up with technology advances is to fund students rather than schools. After the Arizona Supreme Court struck down a voucher program for foster and disabled children under the state's Blaine Amendment, the Goldwater Institute proposed an innovative idea called education savings accounts. For any eligible student who leaves the public schools, the state each year deposits the student's share of state education spending in an account owned by the student's family. The accounts can be used for any educational expense, from private school tuition to distance learning, computer software, tutors, community college classes, and discrete public school services. Any money remaining can be saved for college.

Source: Immigration Wars, by Jeb Bush, p.193, March 5, 2013

School choice is about unions versus kids

There are many people who say they support strong schools but draw the line at school choice. "Sorry, kid. Giving you equal opportunity would be too risky. And it will upset powerful political forces that we need to win elections."

I have a simple message for these masters of delay and deferral: Choose. You can either help the politically powerful unions. Or you can help the kids. Now, I know it's hard to take on the unions. They fund campaigns. But you and I know who deserves a choice.

Source: Republican National Convention speech, Aug. 29, 2012

NOTE: *'Vouchers' are a means of implementing school choice—parents are given a 'voucher' by the school district, which entitles them to, say, $4,000 applicable to either public school or private school tuition. The value of the voucher is generally lower than the cost of one year of public education (which averages $5,200), so private schools (where tuition averages $8,500) may require cash payment in addition to the voucher.*

Rand Paul on Social Security Privatization

Raise retirement age gradually; allow opting out

With regard to entitlement reform, it has to happen. There isn't any question that it will happen. It's whether we do it gradually in a rational manner, or whether we wait until there's a collapse of the country and we have to do it dramatically. Everybody knows the answer. I said it in my campaign. The Republicans attacked me for it and so did the Democrats. The age of Social Security will have to gradually rise. I got a note from a young man who worked in the campaign, and he may be here today. He said, thanks for proposing the $500 billion in budget cuts, thanks for tackling the Social Security problem and then, I wouldn't mind opting out of Social Security. Is there anybody here who would like to opt out of Social Security?

We need bold leadership. We can't have this incrementalism. It's not going to be enough. You need bold leaders who will stand up & say, this should be done in Washington, but this should be left to states and localities respectively. One person can make a difference.

Source: Speech at Conservative Political Action Conference, Feb. 11, 2011

I've never challenged constitutionality of Social Security

Jack Conway (D-KY) is the public face of a new push led by the Progressive Change Campaign Committee that is targeting GOP candidates who support privatizing or cutting Social Security. "Rand Paul, the Tea Party leader running against me for Senate in Kentucky, thinks Social Security is unconstitutional," Conway says in a letter to supporters of the progressive group.

It's a claim that Paul denied as recently as Sunday night: "I've never challenged it and I do not challenge the constitutionality of it," Paul said at a debate.

Source: ABC News coverage of Kentucky Senate debate, Oct. 18, 2010

Jeb Bush on Social Security Privatization

Privatization became administration's fundamental philosophy

The governor sought to extend the use of privatization, and adopted the theory as the fundamental philosophical principle of his administration. He declared, "I would look at any outsource opportunity."

The governor was extraordinarily successful in achieving his legislative goals regarding privatization: Florida hired private sector companies to administer programs that other states had also privatized: managing state prisons, collecting fees on the state's tollways, and cleaning state buildings. But Bush expanded privatization into uncharted territory and contracted out state personnel services (payroll, benefits, training, recruitment, etc.), the management of Medicaid billing.

Like other officials throughout the nation, Bush argued that he was privatizing Florida state government in order to bring about cost savings and efficiency. However, the speed and manner in which he initiated and carried out his plans led some to suggest that political philosophy was the driving force.

Source: Aggressive Conservatism in Florida, by Robert Crew, p.116-7, Dec. 11, 2009

Wrong to scare seniors about not protecting Social Security

A statement from former Florida governor Jeb Bush on Charlie Crist's dishonest Social Security attack on Marco Rubio: "Charlie Crist should be ashamed of his false attack against Marco Rubio on Social Security. Charlie Crist is purposely trying to scare seniors in order to win votes. "The fact is, Marco Rubio will protect Social Security. His own mother relies on Social Security and he has repeatedly stated that he would not support or propose any benefit reductions for current retirees or people who are close to retirement."

Source: John McCormack, The Weekly Standard, "Jeb Rips Crist," Oct. 5, 2010

Rand Paul on Welfare Reform

Federal "gifts" don't generate wealth but perpetuate poverty

Those of us who are actively pursuing the American Dream simply want government to get out of our way. For those of us who feel separated and distant from the American Dream, we don't want be perpetually talked down to, forgotten, and left in perpetual poverty. Many are discouraged that the "gifts" offered by liberals have not generated wealth, but rather perpetuated poverty. People want a way out—not fake concern and baubles.

The war on poverty is 50 years old, and still black unemployment is twice that of white unemployment. Income inequality has worsened under this Administration, and tonight President Obama offers more of the same policies—policies that have allowed the poor to get poorer, and the rich to get richer.

Pitting one American against another is not a pathway towards prosperity. The President is intent on redistributing the pie but not growing it. He misunderstands that the bulk of America wants a bigger pie. They want to work and don't want a handout—but a hand up.

Source: Tea Party response to the State of the Union, Jan. 20, 2015

Poverty line is $11,490, but welfare adds $25,000

The definition of the "poverty line" for a single individual in the United States is $11,490. This certainly isn't very much to live on, but according to the Senate Budget Committee, this individual may qualify for up to $25,000 in various forms of federal welfare. In addition to the salary, welfare benefits would put this individual at more than 300 percent above the poverty line.

[One pundit wrote], "Today 99% of Americans living below the poverty line have electricity, water, flushing toilets, and a refrigerator; 95% have a television; 88% have a telephone; 715 have a car; and 70% have air-conditioning. This may not seem like much, but one hundred years ago men like Henry Ford and Cornelius Vanderbilt were among the richest on the planet, but they enjoyed few of these luxuries."

A Clear Vision to Revitalize America, by Rand Paul, p. 29-30, Oct. 1, 2013

Jeb Bush on Welfare Reform

Taking welfare should be more shameful than working

Aristotle created a special category of virtue, which he called "quasi virtues." In it he placed shame. Shame has always been an important mechanism for exercising self-control.

An example of how we have come to devalue shame in our society is in our welfare system. In the mid-1960s, only half of those eligible for welfare payments were taking them and many enrolled would refuse to take the maximum allowance. People shined shoes and found other ways to bring in money that by today's standards would be considered shameful. However, by the early 1970s, the stigma of receiving welfare had been lost by an administration that encouraged receipt of welfare. The rolls exploded as a much higher percentage of those who were eligible suddenly thought it less shameful to take advantage of the benefits rather than employ themselves in a job requiring hard work, such as shining shoes or sweeping floors. For many it is more shameful to work than to take public assistance-that is how backward shame has become!

Source: Profiles in Character, by Jeb Bush, p. 52-55, Nov. 1, 1995

Vision for a right-to-rise society

Jeb Bush outlined his vision for a "right to rise society," tying it to Detroit's emergence from financial crisis and bankruptcy. In remarks designed to show it's possible for conservative Republicans to care about urban centers, Bush brought to mind the "compassionate conservatism" espoused by his brother, ex-President George W. Bush.

Bush told listeners at the Detroit Economic Club that they "are part of a great story—the revival of a city that means so much to all Americans." Bush continued, "In these past few years, when confronted with grave challenges, you have seized the opportunity to reform the city you love. And you have begun to repair the damage done by decades of mismanagement and empty promises."

Source: Detroit News, "Right-to-rise society," Feb. 4, 2015

Rand Paul on Faith-Based Organizations

Block grant welfare to states and communities

Education, housing, and local commerce, among many other welfare programs for citizens should be the responsibility and role of the states and communities. Through reform ideas like block granting, we can provide federally assisted funds to local communities to help them facilitate and tend to those in need of such essentials such as food or health care. Such proposals would return the responsibility back to the states and promote the opportunity for states to innovate and plan based on the needs of their constituency. Most importantly, it would encourage states to take a more direct look at who is in poverty, who is receiving unnecessary aid, and to facilitate a lessened dependency on government.

Source: A Clear Vision to Revitalize America, by Rand Paul, p. 30-31 , Oct 1, 2013

Economic freedom zones in high unemployment areas

I'm not against having unemployment insurance. I promoted the economic freedom zones which would dramatically lower taxes in areas where there's long-term unemployment. What I would like to do is:

If we extend unemployment insurance, we pay for it. But we add something to it that would create jobs. And so what I have been promoting are economic freedom zones, which any area that has unemployment one-and-a-half times the national average, we would dramatically lower taxes to try to spur and stimulate the economy there and create jobs.

Source: ABC This Week interview, Jan. 11, 2014

NOTE: *"Block grants" refer to transferring unallocated federal funding to the state government, as a means for the state to decide on the content of poverty programs while the federal government decides only the funding amount. Calling for "block grants" means the same as calling for "devolution to the states"; conservatives suggest doing so for many social programs.*

Jeb Bush on Faith-Based Organizations

Welcome faith based organizations as partners

Last year, I asked you to join me in an unshakable commitment to educating our children, diversifying our economy, and strengthening the bonds that hold our families together. We are stronger because we recognize that government isn't the sole answer to the most important questions, and we welcome community and faith based organizations as partners to serve the needs of Florida families. Florida is in a better position to serve our people and face our future, and I thank the members of the Legislature for creating that opportunity.

Source: State of the State speech to the Florida Legislature, March 2, 2004

Created Governor's Faith-Based Advisory Board

Governor Bush embraced the use of religious organizations to take over activities traditionally provided by governmental agencies. To pursue his strategy, Bush created in the Office of the Governor a Faith-Based Advisory Board designed to mobilize additional religious organizations and to encourage their participation in his efforts to make nongovernmental organizations the primary mechanism for delivering public services in Florida. The board also provided direction to state agencies in their use of religious organizations in their work and technical assistance to the organizations in securing grant funds from both the federal and state governments. Bush also required state agencies to create official positions—called faith-based liaisons—to help eliminate internal obstacles to the receipt of funding for religious groups.

Source: Aggressive Conservatism in Florida, by Robert Crew, p. 34, Dec. 11, 2009

NOTE: *President George W. Bush initiated the White House Office of Faith-based and Neighborhood Partnerships to institute his Charitable Choice proposal. Churches are tax-exempt, and donations to churches and other charities are tax-deductible; Pres. Bush's policy was intended to encourage churches to perform more social services. Proponents focus on removing restrictions on religious organizations' activities, so that churches can bid on government block grants for performing welfare services. Opponents claim that lessens restrictions on separation of church and state.*

Rand Paul vs. Jeb Bush on Social Issues

Social issues focus on matters which are based primarily on moral values. Jeb and Rand are both moderates on social issues. These are the issues that the religious conservatives on the right, and the progressives on the left, care deeply about (the Tea Party generally stays silent on social issues). Jeb and Rand agree with the religious conservatives on social issues, more or less, but both are willing to compromise. If you are a religious conservative and want a firebrand on social issues, that firebrand is neither Jeb nor Rand. In other words, the GOP primary invites a religious conservative on these issues: both Rand and Jeb are sensitive to this issue and rhetorically cater to the religious right on these issues. This chapter including the following sections:

- *Abortion (pp. 110-115):* including embryonic stem cell research, contraception, adoption, and state-level restrictions. This topic has always been the most viewed topic on our website www.OnTheIssues.org, so we explore several aspects. Jeb and Rand both oppose abortion on moral grounds; both would restrict family planning advice. On embryonic stem cell research (on which President George W. Bush applied a compromise solution of funding only existing stem cell lines but disallowing new stem cell lines), both Jeb and Rand oppose all federal funding. Abortion-related issues will likely be more relevant in the Republican primaries than in the general election, because Jeb and Rand are both less-than-extreme on this most extreme of issues.

- *Gay Rights (pp. 116-121):* including same-sex marriage at both the state and federal levels. Jeb has "evolved" on gay marriage ("evolved" is the latest euphemism for "changed his mind"): from fully anti-gay marriage in the 1990s to accepting some recognition of some basic rights (but not marriage) now. Rand agrees; this issue also invites a more hard-core primary challenger who has *not* "evolved" at all and strongly opposes any gay rights. To be fair, America has "evolved" on gay marriage too: at the beginning of 2004, same-sex couple could not get legally married anywhere in America; at the end of 2014, same-sex marriage is legal in 35 states.

- *Families and Children (pp. 122-127):* This section would include father's rights and how the candidates apply family values to issues like abortion; but Jeb and Rand don't talk about those issues (once again inviting a religious-right primary opponent). Jeb wrote a book that focused on family values: *Profiles in Character* (reviewed on pp. 229-230) tells parents to teach virtue to their kids (excerpt below, p. 125). Jeb applied family values to family issues (like adoption), but not to anything controversial beyond that. While the religious right focuses on family values as a moral issue, Rand uses it as another means of minority outreach, focusing on the strong family values of the Latino community. Jeb agrees, and adds to that outreach his fluent Spanish, explored further in our immigration section on pp. 192-199.

- *Religion and Patriotism (pp. 128-133):* Jeb and Rand differ only in degree on issues like school prayer (Jeb supports restrictions) and on flag-related issues (Rand would cut off foreign aid to flag-burners). Jeb and Rand disagree on the role of faith in their personal lives. Jeb relies on his faith as the basis for much of his political philosophy; Rand hedges on religion. Rand is therefore much more subject than is Jeb to an attack from the religious right on faith issues.

- *Principles and Values (pp. 134-139):* This section includes some possible campaign themes for 2016. The mainstream media will be most interested in Jeb's and Rand's views on partisanship (they both play up bipartisanship and independence), since they both embody partisanship, according to their opponents. We also address family connections in this section, since both Jeb and Rand will rely on past supporters from their political families.

Rand Paul on Social Issues

Jeb Bush on Social Issues

Rand Paul on Abortion

Life begins at conception

Dr. Paul believes life begins at conception. He recognizes the most basic function of government is to protect life. It is unconscionable that government would facilitate the taking of innocent life. Dr. Paul opposes any federal funding for abortion.

Source: Senate campaign website, www.randpaul2010.com, "Issues," July 19, 2010

Thousands of exceptions follow from maternal health

Senator Rand Paul opposes a national law banning same-sex marriage and federal penalties for drug offenders, and said there could be "thousands of exceptions" to any abortion ban. For many of the evangelical Christians and abortion-rights opponents who dominate Iowa's Republican presidential caucuses, the traditional first round of primary season voting, those positions are unacceptable.

In Paul's view, human life begins at conception and should be granted legal protection from that moment on, although he muddied his message with a March 19 CNN interview where he said that as a physician he could see where there could be "thousands of exceptions" that could make abortion legal. An aide later clarified that Paul meant that a singular exception to save the life of the mother would likely cover thousands of medically different individual cases.

Source: John McCormick on Bloomberg.com, "Rand Paul Cuts Own Path," May 10, 2013

Jeb Bush on Abortion

No need to teach about abortion if we have moral absolutes

Virtues are standards of behavior that are fixed & firm in any civilized society. Who would argue that fortitude, prudence, justice, temperance, discipline, work, responsibility, honesty, honor & compassion are not good things? Listen to William Bennett:

> Forming good character in young people does not mean having to instruct them on thorny issues like abortion, creationism, homosexuality, or euthanasia, to name just a few. People of character can be conservative and good people can be liberal.

Virtues are agreed-upon standards of right and wrong. Values, on the other hand, refer to a system of beliefs possessed by certain groups. Even Nazis and the worst street gangs have values. Since values focus on a position, they tend to accentuate our differences. Modern values often trump traditional values such as accountability, moderation, and deferred gratification. We have all seen the value of personal choice warring against the value of commitment to the family and children.

Source: Profiles in Character, by Jeb Bush, pp. 36-37 ,Nov 1, 1995

OpEd: Jeb avoids extremism on women's issues

The 2012 election cycle has been characterized by an almost obsessive focus on women's reproductive rights. But, amid the chaos, there is still more than one party heavyweight that believes the party's position on women's medical decisions needs to catch up to the modern age. Jeb Bush acknowledged that some conservatives' rather extreme rhetoric on some issues relating to women and minorities is understandably repelling those two groups from the Republican Party.

"I'm concerned about it over the long haul for sure. Our demographics are changing and we have to change not necessarily our core beliefs, but the tone of our message and the intensity of it, for sure," Bush said.

Source: Ashley Portero in International Business Times, Aug. 28, 2012

Rand Paul on Family Planning

Supports religious freedom to deny contraceptive coverage

Sen. Paul today issued the following statement after the Supreme Court's ruling sided with Hobby Lobby on the contraception mandate: "Today, the Supreme Court ruled in favor of religious freedom by taking a stand with Hobby Lobby. Religious liberty will remain intact and all Americans can stay true to their faith without fear of big government intervention or punishment," Sen. Paul said. "Our nation was founded on the principle of freedom, and with this decision, America will continue to serve as a safe haven for those looking to exercise religious liberty."

Source: Senate press release, "Hobby Lobby," June 30, 2014

Supports "Plan B" morning-after contraception

[During an appearance at the College of Charleston], a young woman in the audience asked if Paul, who sponsored an anti-abortion bill in 2013 that defines life as beginning at fertilization, is opposed to Plan B, the emergency contraception commonly known as the morning-after pill.

A number of social conservatives—plenty of them in Iowa—have condemned the morning-after pill as an on-demand abortion drug, sometimes confusing the contraceptive with RU-486, which can be used to induce abortion. Noticeably uncomfortable with the question, Paul first gave a terse answer: "I am not opposed to birth control," he said. After a pause, he elaborated. "That's basically what Plan B is. Plan B is taking two birth control pills in the morning and two in the evening, and I am not opposed to that."

Source: CNN.com, "Rand Paul's campus challenge," Oct. 3, 2014

NOTE: *Burwell v. Hobby Lobby is a landmark Supreme Court decision allowing corporations to be exempt from providing contraception in their healthcare plan, if its owners religiously object,   and there is a less restrictive means of furthering the law's interest. It is the first time that the court has recognized a for-profit corporation's claim of religious belief. The decision is an interpretation of the Religious Freedom Restoration Act.*

Jeb Bush on Family Planning

Funded adoption counseling, but not abortion counseling

As governor, his entry into this arena came in his first year in office when he was called upon to support legislation permitting the state of Florida to offer a specialty license plate promoting the right-to-life side of the abortion controversy. The plate, containing the message "Choose Life," was available for $20 and the proceeds went to organizations that provided counseling and support to pregnant women "who are committed to placing their children up for adoption" but not to "any agency that is involved in or associated with abortion activities including counseling." Not surprisingly, the pro-choice advocates opposed the legislation. Bush's predecessor, Lawton Chiles, had vetoed the same measure on the grounds that it unnecessarily interjected religion into a public issue. Jeb sided with the pro-life side of this debate and signed the bill into law when it came to his desk.

Source: Aggressive Conservatism in Florida, by Robert Crew, p. 74, Dec. 11, 2009

NOTE: *"Roe v. Wade" refers to the 1973 Supreme Court decision legalizing abortion. The essence of the Roe decision is that Constitutional rights apply only after birth; hence abortion does not breach a person's right to life. States cannot regulate 1st trimester abortions; states can regulate but not ban 2nd trimester abortions; and states can ban 3rd trimester abortions (as many have). In 2014 and 2016, abortion opponents focus on peripheral issues like contraception and parental notification, rather than attempting to overturn Roe directly.*

Rand Paul on Stem Cells

Personhood at conception, including embryonic stem cells

Paul is solidifying his outreach to the religious right by proposing a bill focused on one of his pet issues: granting legal rights and protections to fertilized eggs. Paul has introduced the so-called Life at Conception Act, which would grant "personhood" to fertilized eggs, effectively banning abortion, embryonic stem-cell research, many forms of birth control, and assisted reproductive treatments.

From Library of Congress: S.583 & H.R.1091: Life at Conception Act: Sponsored by Sen. Rand Paul along with 132 House members. Introduced 3/12/2013: Declares that the right to life guaranteed by the Constitution is vested in each human being beginning at the moment of fertilization, cloning, or other moment at which an individual comes into being. Prohibits construing this Act to authorize the prosecution of any woman for the death of her unborn child.

Source: RH Reality Check April 8, 2013 coverage of Life at Conception Act,
introduced March 12, 2013

Jeb Bush on Stem Cells

Prevent use of public funds for stem cell research

Governor Bush took the side of the right-to-life constituency in a battle to prevent the use of public funds in support of stem cell research. While this stance put him at odds with his economic development supporters, he argued that this technology "takes a life to give a life," and opposed a ballot initiative that would have amended the state's constitution to provide $200 million over 10 years for this purpose. He also opposed actions to permit the Scripps Medical Institute to conduct research on this topic, even though he had committed $310 million of state-controlled federal funds to attract Scripps to Florida. At the same time he was attempting to lure the Burnham Institute of La Jolla, California, to build a lab in Florida, he also attached a condition that the Florida labs of this company, which was a leader in embryonic stem cell research, could work only on the noncontroversial stem cells from adults or umbilical cords.

Source: Aggressive Conservatism in Florida, by Robert Crew, p. 75, Dec. 11, 2009

Notes: *Stem cells are undifferentiated cells, which are useful in disease research. Stem cells are best taken from human fetuses; hence the pro-life opposition. Many pro-life advocates support fetal stem cell research because of the medical potential. In 2001, Pres. George W. Bush announced that the federal policy would be to allow fetal stem cell research on existing stem cell lines but not on new ones.*

In March 2009, Pres. Obama ended the ban on funding embryonic stem cell research. In signing the executive order, Obama said: "When it comes to stem cell research, rather than furthering discovery, our government has forced into what I believe is a false choice between sound science and moral values. In this case, I believe the two are not inconsistent."

Rand Paul on Gay Rights

I don't believe in rights based on your behavior

Sen. Rand Paul said he doesn't buy into the concept of gay rights because they are defined by a gay person's lifestyle: "I don't think I've ever used the term 'gay rights,' because I don't really believe in rights based on your behavior," Paul told reporters in a videotaped interview that has received little attention since it was recorded in 2013.

But it's unclear how far—and to whom—Paul extends the argument that rights cannot be defined by behavior. Practicing religion, for example, is a behavior enshrined in the Bill of Rights, as is the behavior of free speech. Does Paul believe those behaviors are protected rights?

A Paul spokesperson said the rights that count are those in the country's founding charter. "He does not classify rights based on behavior, but rather recognizes rights for all, as our Constitution defines it. Sen. Paul is the biggest proponent for protecting the Bill of Rights, which protects the rights of all Americans as stated in our Constitution."

Source: Buzzfeed.com, "Concept of gay rights," March 31, 2015

Make federal benefits equal for gay couples

When Obama came out in support of gay marriage last year, Paul said that he didn't think the president's views "could get any gayer." "I'm an old-fashioned traditionalist," the senator later told National Review. "I believe in the historic and religious definition of marriage."

At the same time, Paul suggests that the tax code and health insurance should be made neutral so that gay couples benefit from the same breaks as married ones. And like Rubio, he has said that gay marriage should be left to the states to decide. He said Sunday that he is okay with the government being "neutral" on gay marriage; in February he said he was "not sure" how he felt about DOMA.

But he's already willing to let other states legalize gay marriage and to let gay couples have some federal benefits; he could expand that to mean marriage in all but name.

Source: Rachel Weiner in Washington Post, March 26, 2013

Jeb Bush on Gay Rights

Gay rights & feminism are "modern victim movements"

Since the 1960s, the politics of victimization has steadily intensified. Being a victim gives rise to certain entitlements, benefits, and preferences in society. The surest way to get something in today's society is to elevate one's status to that of the oppressed. Many of the modern victim movements-the gay rights movement, the feminist movement, the black empowerment movement-have attempted to get people to view themselves as part of a smaller group deserving of something from society.

It is a major deviation from the society envisioned by Martin Luther King, who would have had people judged by the content of their character and not by the color of their skin—or sexual preference or gender or ethnicity. Eventually there will come a time when everybody will be able to claim some status as a victim of society, leaving few in society who will actually be considered the victimizers. Who, then, will be left to blame in a world in which it is victim against victim?

Source: Profiles in Character, by Jeb Bush, pp. 59-60, Nov. 1, 1995

1994: LGBT protections are tantamount to elevating sodomy

A sharply conservative tone came to characterize Bush's entire 1994 gubernatorial campaign. In July, Bush published a now-infamous op-ed arguing against anti-discrimination protections for LGBT people, which he said were tantamount to elevating "sodomy." Bush's team has since sought to distance him from that piece, with a spokeswoman telling BuzzFeed that it "does not reflect Gov. Bush's views now."

Source: New York Times interview, "Evolving Views," Jan. 11, 2015

Rand Paul on Gays in the Military

Military should decide don't-ask-don't-tell policy

Democratic US Senate nominee Jack Conway says gays should be allowed to serve openly in the US military, while his Republican rival, Rand Paul, says the military should decide the issue. Kentucky's US Senate candidates were asked their opinions on the so-called "Don't Ask, Don't Tell" policy in the wake of this week's unsuccessful effort by Democrats in the US Senate to repeal it.

When Conway was asked whether gays and lesbians should be allowed to serve openly in the military, he said "yes," without elaborating.

Paul's campaign spokesman said in an e-mail without elaboration, "Dr. Paul believes this is a matter that should be decided by the leadership of the military, not through political posturing."

Republicans in the US Senate this week stopped a repeal of "Don't Ask, Don't Tell" when Democrats attached an amendment seeking the repeal to a defense bill. Republicans said a Pentagon study on the impact of ending the policy should be completed before there is any move toward repeal.

Source: Lexington Herald-Leader coverage of Kentucky Senate debate, Sep. 23, 2010

NOTE: Pres. Bill Clinton implemented two policies on gay rights as President: "don't ask, don't tell" (DADT) and DOMA (see next page). The policy banning open homosexuals serving in the military was repealed on Sept. 20, 2011. Hence gay and lesbian people may now openly serve in the US military. Since 1993, the DADT policy held that homosexuals may serve as long as they do not announce their homosexuality ("Don't Tell"), but also that the military may not investigate their homosexuality ("Don't Ask"). The policy banning open homosexuals serving in the military was repealed on Sept. 20, 2011. Hence gay and lesbian people may now openly serve in the US military.

Jeb Bush on Gays in the Military

Don't-ask-don't-tell ok if it doesn't affect policy

Jeb Bush was less of a hard-liner when a gay Floridian hoping to win a job in Mr. Bush's administration gently asked if his sexual orientation would present a problem.

"On the other stuff, don't ask, don't tell is fine with me," Mr. Bush responded, appropriating the terminology President Bill Clinton used regarding gays in the military. "What you do in your private life is your business. If it crosses over into the public policy realm, then that is another matter. If you are comfortable with that, then we can proceed."

Source: New York Times, "Bush's Emails as Governor," Dec. 24, 2014

NOTE: *[Gay marriage next page]: Prior to the 2012 election, 13 states allowed same-sex civil unions or had some similar legislation, and 29 states had laws defining marriage as one-man-one-woman. By the 2014 election, the number of states allowing same-sex marriage had risen to 34 states. Several more states have legalized same-sex marriage but it has not yet taken effect (but will by the 2016 election). With a majority of states having legalized same-sex marriage, at issue now is federal law, which includes numerous aspects of federal benefits.*

Rand Paul on Defense of Marriage Act

Don't register guns federally, nor marriages

I asked about same-sex marriage: "I don't want my guns registered in Washington or my marriage," he told me. "The Founding Fathers all got married by going down to the local courthouse. It is a local issue and always has been."

What about rapidly-changing opinions on the matter? He took a soft tone. "Society's changing," he said. "People change their minds all the time on this issue, and even within the Republican Party, there are people whose child turns out to be gay and they're like, 'maybe I want to rethink this issue.' So it's been rethought. The President's rethought the issue. A lot of people have rethought the issue."

Was Paul hinting that he, too, could change his thinking? He said, "I believe in old-fashioned traditional marriage. But, I don't really think the government needs to be too involved with this, and I think that the Republican Party can have people on both sides of the issue."

"You could rethink it at some point, too?" I asked. He shrugged. It wasn't a yes or a no.

Source: Jonathan Martin in New York Times, Dec. 25, 2014

No national law on same-sex marriage; leave it to states

Paul opposes a national law banning same-sex marriage. Paul's view is that same-same marriage should be dealt with at the state level. Paul said he thinks his party and the nation will eventually accept that different parts of the country have different views on certain issues. "My position on this is the same as Thomas Jefferson, Ben Franklin, George Washington, John Adams," he said. "Marriage is a state issue."

Source: John McCormick onBloomberg.com, "Rand Paul Cuts Own Path," May 10, 2013

Jeb Bush on Defense of Marriage Act

Traditional marriage best; but recognize gay couples

Bush believes in traditional marriage, but he supports recognition for gay couples: "I don't think people need to be discriminated against because they don't share my belief on this, and if [gay] people love their children with all their heart and soul, that should be held up as examples for others to follow because we need it," he told Charlie Rose last June. Likewise, he told the conservative CPAC conference earlier this month that "way too many people believe Republicans are anti-everything," including "anti-gay."

Back in 2006 Bush said he was leaning towards support for a constitutional ban on gay marriage in Florida, after previously holding that the ban was unnecessary. (Same-sex marriages were already illegal under state law). But in the gay marriage debate, six years is a long time. Bush seems positioned to move toward gay marriage support if he so chose.

Source: Rachel Weiner in Washington Post, March 26, 2013

No hate-crimes status for gays; no gay marriage

Q: Do you believe that the Florida government should include sexual orientation in Florida's anti-discrimination laws?

A: No.

Q: Do you believe that the Florida government should recognize same-sex marriages?

A: No.

Source: Florida National Political Awareness Test, July 2, 1998

NOTE: *"DOMA" refers to the Defense of Marriage Act, passed by Congress in 1996, which defined marriage as consisting of one man and one woman (in other words, barring same-sex marriage). DOMA applies to all federal benefits and taxes, but not necessarily to state benefits and taxes. On March 27, 2013, the Supreme Court heard US v. Windsor on overturning DOMA.*

Rand Paul on Family Values

Revival of values depends on fusing freedom and virtue

[At the 2014 Values Voter Summit], Paul tried to sell the crowd on how his libertarian politics are necessary for virtue and family values. Paul appeared a bit less at home, standing behind a podium and reading from the teleprompter, and speaking quickly.

Paul—whose libertarian views don't always sync with those of Christian conservatives – said his policies were key to preserving family values: "What American needs is not a politician with more promises, what America really needs is a revival," Paul said, earning his first cheers of the speech. He went on to argue that that the revival depends on fusing freedom and virtue together.

"Liberty is exactly essential to virtue," he said. Paul championed his anti-abortion stance; he was introduced to the crowd by a video montage of his own pro-life remarks interspersed with sonograms of babies in the womb. "I'm one who will march for life and who will stand up in defense of life as long as I'm privileged to hold office," Paul told the crowd. Paul's strongest applause came when he brought up was his failed legislative attempt to stop foreign aid from reaching countries that persecute Christians. "Let's stop this madness!" he said.

Source: By Jane C. Timm on MSNBC.com, "Religious Conservatives"

NOTE: When Democrats discuss family values, they mean economic issues such as child tax deductions and child support; and some moral issues such as internet & TV child filters; and child support. When Republicans discuss family values, they mean a more general concept of traditional American society, hinting at:
- *Traditional roles for women versus men*
- *Traditional marriage over same-sex marriage*
- *Traditional child-rearing concepts like encouraging abstinence*
- *Pro-life and pro-adoption.*

Jeb Bush on Family Values

Pass moral judgment & teach virtue to our children

Correcting our social pathologies will take time. Foremost, it will require a renewal of virtue and character and a rejuvenation of those institutions that teach virtue and character. We need to teach our children that there are universal rights and wrongs, that you can't spend your life explaining away or justifying deviant conduct. This means, then, that we must regain confidence in passing moral judgments, using the language of virtue and teaching virtue to our children.

It is important that we begin to discuss virtue and character in the context of those who exhibit true virtue and character on a routine basis. We must elevate the people who are redefining our culture every day for the better for they are the profiles in character from whom we must learn. Following their lead, we must make a conscious effort to practice even small acts of character and virtue. If we roll up our sleeves and do our part, the answer to our cultural problems will come.

Source: Profiles in Character, by Jeb Bush, pp. 41-42, Nov. 1, 1995

Supper with kids keeps them away from drugs & booze

In 2005, Jeb hosted "Family Day" in the Capitol courtyard to encourage parents to have supper together with their children as a way to stay close and help keep them away from drugs and booze. Family Day took place barely a week after [Jeb's son] Jebbie was arrested for public intoxication in Austin, where he was a senior at the University of Texas.

"Families are the first line of offense and the first line of defense in providing support for children," explained Jeb to a pretty television reporter. "It's common sense. I think everybody would understand how strong, wholesome family life really matters, but there is really data, real research that suggests that families that are united, families that eat together, just have dinner together will have a better chance of their children being drug free and alcohol free."

So I asked Jeb if he wished he had spent more time with his own children. He walked away without saying a word.

Source: America's Next Bush, by S.V. Date, p. 66-67, Feb. 15, 2007

Rand Paul on Latino Family Values

Latinos support GOP stances of faith and family values

Republicans need to become parents of a new future with Latino voters or we will need to resign ourselves to permanent minority status. The Republican Party has insisted for years that we stand for freedom and family values. I am most proud of my party when it stands for both. The vast majority of Latino voters agree with us on these issues but Republicans have pushed them away with harsh rhetoric over immigration.

In our zeal for border control, Republicans have been losing both the respect and votes of a group of people who already identify with our belief in family, faith, and conservative values. Hispanics should be a natural and sizable part of the Republican base. That they have steadily drifted away from the GOP in each election says more about Republicans than it does about Hispanics. Defense of the unborn and defense of traditional marriage are Republican issues that should resonate with Latinos but have been obscured by the misperception that Republicans are hostile to immigrants.

As we move forward on immigration reform, I for one will work to find a solution that both adheres to the rule of law and makes room for compassion. My hope is that today we begin a dialogue between the GOP and Latinos.

Source: Senate press release, "Hispanics natural GOP," June 12, 2013

Jeb Bush on Latino Family Values

Conservatives and Hispanics share family values

Certainly the most important characteristics most conservatives and Hispanics share are religious and family values. What is most striking about Hispanic religious beliefs is their attachment to "renewalist" faiths—Pentecostal, evangelical, and charismatic: 2/3 of Hispanics say their religious beliefs are an important influence on their political thinking.

But conservatism among religious Hispanics has not translated into Republican partisan affiliation. Democrats outnumber Republicans by 55 to 18% among Hispanic Catholics, compared to a 39 to 32% Republican edge among non-Hispanic Catholics. Republicans should make an effort to connect with Hispanics on religious faith and moral values.

Source: Immigration Wars, by Jeb Bush, p.219-220, March 5, 2013

NOTE: *In the 2016 elections, the concept of "Latino family values" may play an important role in the Republican primaries. Numerous surveys support that Latinos support the Republican definition of traditional family values, yet they vote overwhelmingly Democratic in presidential elections. Some Republicans, especially Gov. Jeb Bush (R-FL) and Sen. Rand Paul (R-KY), have both focused on how to reach Latinos on grounds of shared family values, to overcome the demographic problem of the overwhelming Democratic vote. A full analysis of Latino demographics in the presidential election appears on p. 171.*

Rand Paul on Foster Care Policy

Re-establish inter-country adoptions from Guatemala

Guatemalan President Otto Perez Molina agreed in a meeting with Sen. Paul to review his country's strict policies that have prevented Americans from adopting impoverished children from Guatemala. Paul noted, "For years, there would be tens of thousands of kids who would be adopted each year in our country and it's dwindled almost to nothing." If the recent adoption policy were reversed, "maybe that would take pressure off of some of the people, particularly unattended minors, from coming [illegally]," he added.

Paul relayed to Molina that if Guatemala fixes the issues of the Hague Adoption Convention's inconsistency with Guatemalan law, it could pave the way for willing U.S. families to adopt Guatemalan children. The effect could be reduced pressure for children to travel hundreds of miles illegally to the U.S., in many cases dying en route.

In January 2008, Guatemala shut down all intercountry adoptions. Paul noted, "There were thousands of kids being adopted from Guatemala until 2009, and then it's dwindled. They've cleared some of the backlog, and they said it used to be maybe too easy and now it's way too hard but there could be a legal way to try to improve immigration this way. But with regards to immigration, I let him know I don't think the source of the problem is in Guatemala. It's in our White House."

Paul said adoption policy changes in Guatemala are hardly the main cause of the border crisis and that the root issue is President Obama's immigration policy.

Source: Matthew Boyle on Breitbart.com, Aug. 21, 2014

Jeb Bush on Foster Care Policy

No Place Like Home initiative: find families for DCF kids

We must do our part to find families for children who need them, by finding permanent homes for the children in state care. There are more than 4,000 children in Department of Children & Families care today. In November, we launched the *No Place Like Home* initiative to find Florida families who will open their hearts and homes to them.

We're actively looking for the right families, and streamlining the adoption process to remove the obstacles and frustrations that have been part of the process for far too long. We are committed to supporting Florida's families, but government will never be the full answer to their needs. Our state is blessed with an incredibly strong network of community and faith-based partners that offer a helping hand, provide counseling, and teach skills required to build strong families and hold them together.

Source: State of the State speech to the Florida Legislature, March 2, 2004

Parental consent over government intrusions into families

While I support the idea of providing comprehensive services for the early identification and intervention of learning disabilities, I have a number of concerns with Senate Bill 1018, grounded on the potential for excessive intrusiveness of government in the lives of Florida's families.

- The bill is silent on the issue of parental consent for referral, assessment and intervention services for identified children and their families. Referrals of "high risk children" are automatic and may be interpreted to be without parental consent.
- The absence of a public records exemption to protect the privacy of families and children impacted is also problematic.
- The Florida State Laboratory will be required to purchase an expensive piece of equipment to process required Tandem Mass Spectrometry tests of all newborns.
- And finally, this program is to be provided at an enormous cost to taxpayers, despite services already provided by the state.

Source: Veto notification on Senate Bill 1018, May 31, 2001

Rand Paul on Freedom of Religion

US aid enables a war on Christianity in the Middle East

Before the Arab Spring, Christianity flourished in small outposts, like the Coptic Christians in Egypt. I had hoped that the Arab Spring would bring freedom to long-oppressed people throughout the Middle East, but I fear the Arab Spring is becoming an Arab winter.

Today, Christians in Iraq, Libya, Egypt and Syria are on the run—persecuted or under fire—and yet, we continue to send aid to the folks chasing them. While they burn the American flag and the mobs chant "Death to America," more of your money is sent to these haters of Christianity.

Even if all the atrocities to Christians were not occurring in these countries, we simply don't have the money to engage in this foolishness. We must borrow the money from China to send it to Pakistan.

It is clear that American taxpayer dollars are being used to enable a war on Christianity in the Middle East and I believe that must end.

Source: Faith & Freedom Coalition speech, June 13, 2013

NOTE (opposite page): *Current law is that schools allow religious groups to organize on school grounds as if they are any club. Schools are not allowed to conduct prayers at the beginning of school, but neither are they allowed to stop a student from praying.*

Jeb Bush on Freedom of Religion

Let businesses express religious freedom

Bush opened up a bit about his Catholic faith and religious freedom laws. He embraced Indiana Gov. Mike Pence's recent signing of a controversial religious-freedom law calling it "the right thing" to do. The legislation has sparked intense backlash from Democrats and gay-rights groups, but Bush noted that President Clinton had signed a similar measure two decades ago. "This is simply allowing people of faith space to be able to express their beliefs, to be able to be people of conscience," Bush said. "I just think, once the facts are established, people aren't going to see this as discriminatory at all."

In recent weeks, some of Bush's biggest skeptics in the faith community had specifically mentioned wanting to hear from Bush on the issue of religious liberties. His comments put him publicly in line with the conservative evangelical right that he is quietly wooing.

Source: National Journal, "Jeb Bush Interview," March 30, 2015

School prayer OK if prayers are voluntary and student-led

No longer faced with a sure-fire veto by the governor, a Republican-heavy group of lawmakers is resurrecting a controversial school-prayer bill for the first time in three years. "Children should be allowed to pray if they choose to so long as all religions are respected and it's not during class time," said one state Representative. State law permits public schools to offer secular Bible or religion study as an extracurricular activity, but the House measure would allow students to lead a public, nonsectarian prayer at graduations, school athletic events and some assemblies.

The measure is virtually identical to a bill that made it through the Legislature in 1996 but was killed by then-Gov. Lawton Chiles, a Democrat who vowed to veto any future school-prayer legislation that crossed his desk. In Gov. Jeb Bush, though, the Legislature now at least has a willing ear. Bush has said he would consider school-prayer legislation if the prayers were voluntary and student-led.

Source: Karla Schuster in Orlando Sentinel, "School Prayer,"
March 20, 1999

Rand Paul on Flag Issues

End US aid to countries that burn our flag

Sen. Paul told conservatives gathered at CPAC that ending foreign aid to nations like Egypt rather than stopping school children from touring the White House is a better way to cut federal spending: "I say not one penny more to countries that are burning our flag," Paul said, as the crowd rose to its feet and cheered. He chided the president for halting the tours as a way to deal with the across-the-board federal budget cuts required by the Budget Control Act, or sequester, which was proposed and signed into law by the president.

"The president's He's trying to do his fair share," Paul said. "But within a few days, the president finds an extra $250 million dollars to send to Egypt." Paul was referring to money appropriated by Congress to help the new government in Egypt where protests against the US have included burning the America flag, and "where mobs attacked out embassy and chanted 'death to America,' [but Obama] found an extra $250 million to reward them," Paul said.

Source: CNSnews.com coverage of Conservative Political Action Conference, March 14, 2013

NOTE: *The flag desecration amendment is considered a proxy issue for free speech (if you oppose the amendment) or a proxy issue for patriotism (if you support the amendment). A flag-desecration law was introduced in every Congress from 1995 to 2006; it passed the House in each session, and failed to pass the Senate by only one vote in 2005. A flag-desecration bill has been sponsored in both the House and Senate (without a vote) in every Congress from 2007 to 2013.*

Jeb Bush on Flag Issues

Removed Confederate battle flag from Florida Capitol

Jeb unceremoniously banished the "Stainless Banner"—a small Confederate battle flag on an otherwise white field—from the grounds of the Florida Capitol. Previously it had flown along with all the others flags that Florida had flown under in the five centuries since Europeans arrived.

There was no announcement, no nothing. The official reasoning, released after the fact, was that the flagpoles had all been taken down anyway for some renovation work on that side of the building, and, when it was over, it was decided that the Confederate flag would not go back up. Simple as that. Passive voice construction—"it was decided"—and that was the end of it.

No one really noticed, in fact, until the local papers got a complaint from the head of the Sons of the Confederacy, the self-described nonracist group that is merely interested in preserving Southern heritage. To his credit, Jeb did not back down. He didn't even waste much breath defending his decision. The action spoke for itself.

Source: America's Next Bush, by S.V. Dáte, p.195, Feb. 15, 2007

Rand Paul on Personal Faith

I am a Christian but not always a good one

I'm a Christian, a husband and a father. I'm faithful to my wife and my family. I try to be good at all those things, though, of course, we all fall short of perfection in our lives. I try to adhere to the tenets of God's word in the New Testament. I take seriously my oath to defend the Constitution. And I try to fight for truth and my values regardless of the political outcome, regardless of how popular or unpopular they may be.

Dostoevsky wrote that I did not arrive at my hosanna through childlike faith, but through a fiery furnace of doubt. My faith has never been easy for me, never been easy to talk about and never been without obstacles. I do not and cannot wear my religion on my sleeve. I am a Christian but not always a good one. I'm not completely free of doubts. I struggle to understand man's inhumanity to man. I struggle to understand the horrible tragedies that war inflicts on our young men and women.

My faith has never been easy for me, never been easy to talk about and never been without obstacles. I do not and cannot wear my religion on my sleeve. I am a Christian but not always a good one. I'm not completely free of doubts. I struggle to understand man's inhumanity to man. I struggle to understand the horrible tragedies that war inflicts on our young men and women.

Source: Speech at Values Voters Summit, Sept. 14, 2012

Jeb Bush on Personal Faith

9/11/2001: after emergency meeting, went to church to pray

On Sep. 11, 2001, Jeb answered the expected questions about what the state would be doing to guard against new attacks. And finally someone asked where Jeb was going next. With the familiar, pinched grin, Jeb told us: "I'm going to Mass."

Something like that, on a day like that, there should have been absolutely no reason for it not to ring true. And yet...it was somehow off, just a little bit. He knew that whatever he said was likely to be widely reported. He was going to Mass. He was a good Catholic, and in a time of trouble, he was seeking solace in prayer.

Why the need to get this message out? Because unlike his brother, Jeb had never been a particularly public Christian. It was more important to be a Christian, in the immediate aftermath of September 11, in the high-contrast, Christianity-versus-Islam worldview that set in.

Source: America's Next Bush, by S.V. Dáte, p.303-304, Feb. 15, 2007

Focus on virtue & character, not values

We must do a better job of instilling character and virtue in our children and helping those institutions charged with this task. It means not getting bogged down in the current and unwinnable debate over values. That debate must be redefined in the context of virtues.

Values have replaced virtues as our moral lighthouses, and there are many different value systems present in our culture. Our character-building institutions have bought into the idea that we have to recognize all kinds of value systems and, instead of providing us guidance, now provide us with tools to justify a wide variety of deviant behaviors. In other words, they do not teach our children right from wrong, but rather how to make informed choices.

Our children need direction, not choices. If we give them the proper direction, the principles by which to live their lives, then in the long run they will be more likely to make the right choices. We must become more virtue oriented and less value oriented.

Source: Profiles in Character, by Jeb Bush, p. 21 & 35, Nov. 1, 1995

Rand Paul on Principles & Values

We don't need new principles, just to stand by those we have

SEN. MARCO RUBIO (video clip): We don't need a new idea. There is an idea. The idea is called America. And it still works.

Q: Is that enough? America still works?

PAUL: Well, I don't think we need new principles. I think the principles we have, we need to be more explicit with. And, instead of saying, "oh, we want revenue-neutral tax reform," I think we need to stand up and say, "we want to leave more money in the economy. We want to reduce taxes—that when Reagan did it, we had 7% growth in one year." That's the kind of bold leadership we need but it's not a new principle. We don't have to reinvent ourselves in that way, but we do have to stand on principle. And unless you really stand for something, people aren't motivated to go out and vote for you.

Source: Fox News Sunday interview, March 24, 2013

Politicians should apply medical oath: "First, do no harm"

As a physician, I was taught first to do no harm: To think before you act, to analyze the unintended consequences of your actions. I think America would be better off if all our politicians took that same approach: "First, do no harm." It is self-evident that the President and Congress are unable to do what every family in America must do—balance the budget.

Source: Tea Party response to the State of the Union, Jan. 20, 2015

Jeb Bush on Principles & Values

America is different because identity derives from ideals

American is different from any other country on earth in many ways, but most significant is that our national identity derives not from a common ethnicity but from a set of ideals—not just life, liberty, and the pursuit of happiness, but individualism, faith, family, community, democracy, tolerance, equal opportunity, individual responsibility, and freedom of enterprise. Those ideals are set forth in our nation's founding documents and enmeshed in its institutions.

But though our nation was founded on those ideals and continues largely to hold fast to them, America does not hold a monopoly over them. Quite to the contrary, millions of people around the world cherish those ideals and strive toward becoming Americans.

Source: Immigration Wars, by Jeb Bush, p. 69, March 5, 2013

1994 and 1998 campaign theme: Think outside the box

With Jeb, Floridians in 1994 & 1998 were told they were getting a Bush who, despite his family, was his own man. He was a thinker, a "searcher," Jeb told us. Someone who would think outside the box. Should he run for the presidency, this idea will become a main theme for his campaign, the number one talking point, at least at first, to open as much space as possible between the Jeb the Serious and Curious Grown-up and George the Perpetual Frat-boy Adolescent.

A decade and a half after his first appearance in statewide politics, it became clear that there was some truth to the original sales pitch. Jeb does seem more thoughtful and analytical than his father had been, and is obviously much more so than his older brother. But to focus on these differences downplays a far more important truth: that Jeb's agenda and his views on most major topics are virtually identical to that of his father and brother, with at best minor refinements.

Source: America's Next Bush, by S.V. Dáte, p. 27, Feb. 15, 2007

Rand Paul on Partisanship

My victory was part of a much larger Tea Party movement

"I have a message from the Tea Party, a message that is loud and clear and does not mince words. We've come to take our government back." Speaking these words after winning Kentucky's Republican primary in spring 2012, I understood that my victory was part of a much larger movement. Voters outraged by massive debt, spending and an out-of-control federal government had elected a candidate the media and political establishment had deemed too unconventional—precisely because they desired a more unconventional politics. The status quo had failed. Big government had failed. On that warm May evening, Kentucky voters sent a message loud and clear: We've had enough.

Source: The Tea Party Goes to Washington, by Rand Paul, p. xi, Feb. 22, 2011

Elect lovers of liberty, not just Republicans

Imagine with me for a moment, imagine a time when liberty is again spread from coast to coast. Imagine a time when our great country is again governed by the Constitution. Imagine a time when the White House is once again occupied by a friend of liberty. You may think I'm talking about electing Republicans. I'm not. I'm talking about electing lovers of liberty.

It isn't good enough to pick the lesser of two evils. We must elect men and women of principle, and conviction and action, who will lead us back to greatness. There is a great and tumultuous battle underway for the future, not of the Republican Party but the future of the entire country.

Will you, America's next generation of liberty lovers, will you stand and be heard? There's a battle going on. Don't forget, there is a great battle going on for the heart and soul of America. The Fourth Amendment is equally as important as the Second Amendment, and conservatives cannot forget this.

Source: Speech at CPAC convention, March 8, 2014

Jeb Bush on Partisanship

GOP isn't about orthodoxy & disallowing disagreement

I asked Jeb there about the Republican Party. "Ronald Reagan would have, based on his record of finding accommodation, finding some degree of common ground, as would my dad—they would have a hard time if you define the Republican Party—and I don't—as having an orthodoxy that doesn't allow for disagreement, doesn't allow for finding some common ground," Bush said, adding that he views the hyper-partisan moment as "temporary."

"Back to my dad's time and Ronald Reagan's time—they got a lot of stuff done with a lot of bipartisan support," he said. Reagan "would be criticized for doing the things that he did."

In the 12 years(!) since he last ran for office, Bush missed the rise of the tea party, and the ascendancy of a new generation of politicians— Marco Rubio, Paul Ryan, Scott Walker, Ted Cruz, among them. Those men occasionally, carefully, respectfully break with the movement. Scorning today's Republican Party is, by contrast, the core of Jeb's political identity.

Source: Ben Smith on BuzzFeed.com, "Terrible Candidate," April 7, 2014

Obama divided into "them vs. us"; GOP needs alternatives

Q: What do you mean when you say Obama won by "dividing the country"?

BUSH: The basic part of his campaign was that those who were successful weren't paying their fair share, even though we have incredibly high taxes for high-income Americans. He ran a campaign of "them and us." And it was quite effective: that somehow Republicans don't care about the large number of people. And it's not true. But in order to win, I think Republicans need to offer a compelling alternative and have proposals on health care, on tax reform, on entitlement reform.

Source: CBS Face the Nation, March 10, 2013

Rand Paul on Family Connections

Being Ron Paul's son means being unique-minded independent

I remain very much my father's son, not only in my politics but in the way that Dad and I have different approaches to things. It really shouldn't surprise people that part of being Ron Paul's son means being your own man, independent and unique-minded. If I blindly followed Dad with no differences of opinion I would be less my father's son, not more. Dad and I have always understood this even when others have not. My father's popularity and influence have been a tremendous help to my political career. I don't think I could have become a Senator without him but, for most of my life and certainly my political life, I have never been dependent on my dad—and he wouldn't have it any other way.

While many now look to my father as a champion of liberty, let's just say I caught the liberty bug much earlier and, yes, I admit I had a particular advantage. As a child, when people would come over to the house and start political discussions, I was always very comfortable with the adult conversation.

*Source: The Tea Party Goes to Washington, by Rand Paul, pp. 27-8,
Feb. 22, 2011*

Wife Kelley gave Randal Paul his nickname "Rand"

As for my name, growing up I always went by Randy, but even early on, when we were just dating, Kelley didn't think it fit me. She would always say, "You just don't sound like a Randy." She thought Randal was too formal and would simply call me Rand. I liked it. More important, Kelley liked it, and so it was pretty much settled.

*Source: The Tea Party Goes to Washington, by Rand Paul, p. 36,
Feb 22, 2011*

NOTE: *Many Libertarians assume that Rand Paul is named after Ayn Rand, the leading Objectivist philosopher who provides much of the basis for libertarianism. But his Objectivist-sounding nickname was chosen by his wife, not his parents.*

Jeb Bush on Family Connections

Bush family name is a detriment that limits career choices

Jeb Bush's adult pre-political career was spent in Texas, in Venezuela, and in south Florida where most of those who followed his career say that he employed a political and business strategy long familiar to historians of the political dynasty whose name he carries. The strategy was to exploit the Bush family name and to draw on a huge universe of family relationships, family money, and elite contacts in order to propel himself into successful careers in both business and politics. Some saw it as a two-step procedure:

- leverage the Bush family name and a small personal investment into really big money, always provided by others, and

- if any deal goes sour, exit early with personal fortune intact, or rely on a bailout from one of Dad's fairy godfathers."

Not unexpectedly, Jeb took umbrage at the implication that he was not a self-made man and said that the Bush family name was really a detriment to his ambitions and that it limited his career choices.

Source: Aggressive Conservatism in Florida, by Robert Crew, p. 1, Dec 11, 2009

I admire my father & brother, but I am my own man

I have been lucky to have a father and a brother who both have shaped America's foreign policy from the Oval Office. I recognize that as a result, my views will often be held up in comparison to theirs'— sometimes in contrast to theirs'. I love my father and my brother. I admire their service to the nation and the difficult decisions they had to make.

But I am my own man—and my views are shaped by my own thinking and own experiences. Each president learns from those who came before—their principles; their adjustments. One thing we know is this: Every president inherits a changing world, and changing circumstances.

Source: Speech to the Chicago Council on Global Affairs, Feb. 18, 2015

Rand Paul vs. Jeb Bush
on National Security Issues

This chapter focuses on issues of war policy and defense spending, and issues involving foreign nations that may lead to U. S. military action in the future (the following chapter focuses on non-military foreign policy). Rand Paul, as a member of the Senate Foreign Relations Committee and the Senate Homeland Security Committee, has a well-established voting record on national security issues, while Jeb has expressed only limited views.

Jeb's lack of a full set of policy stances in this topic area must be addressed before Jeb hits the hustings in 2016, lest he appear unknowledgeable like Sarah Palin or Herman Cain when they were suddenly confronted with questions on foreign policy topics they had not previously been asked. Jeb has had more time to prepare than did Palin or Cain, so presumably he will surround himself with foreign policy advisors who will ensure that Jeb knows his stuff. Jeb has already begun this process, which we capture in his excerpts below.

Jeb does have some long-standing policy stances in this area, for issues that relate to Florida, such as Cuba and National Guard deployments. And he published a book in 2013 discussing numerous aspects of immigration, including cross-border issues with Mexico (see pp. 192-199). But other than immigration and Florida issues, Jeb's foreign policy stances are still "thin."

When Jeb finally does make a major speech on the missing topics in national security and foreign policy, you can infer two certain outcomes: (1) We will edit this book to produce a new revision with his more complete stances on national security; and (2) Jeb is most certainly running for president.

This chapter includes the following sections:

- *Global War on Terror (pp. 144-151):* This category addresses how Jeb Bush and Rand Paul would take action against terrorism. Both Jeb and Rand blame Hillary Clinton for Benghazi. Jeb also blames President Obama for the rise of the Islamic State, but Rand focuses more on staying out of foreign entanglements. Rand applies the same logic to our September 11th response, warning against nation-building abroad and spying domestically, while Jeb advocates intervention abroad based on 9/11.

- **Middle East (pp. 152-159):** Jeb has made clear that he supports the Iraq War and Afghan War, and takes a hard line against Iran and supporting Israel. Jeb and Rand most differ on this issue: Rand opposed the Iraq War; opposes intervention in Syria or Iran; and opposes intervention against ISIS. Jeb echoes the underlying neoconservative approach of his brother, President George W. Bush, but insists he makes his decisions independently. It is likely that Jeb will be advised on Middle East issues by some of the same neocon advisers who worked for his brother, which may sway him towards the extremes from his more moderate stance.

- **Military Budget (pp. 160-163):** This section concerns defense policy, not war policy: defense spending issues and defense strategy goals. We have to infer Jeb's views on federal defense spending from how he handled Florida's defense spending (pushing to keep military bases open). Rand's Senate votes were libertarian: questioning military spending; questioning over-militarization; as well as questioning U.S. intervention abroad.

- **Political Hotspots (pp. 164-169):** including the current ongoing international disputes in Cuba, Russia and North Korea. Jeb has far fewer opinions that does Rand Paul on these issues, but Jeb is studying, as described in his views on Russia and North Korea below, where he advocates a more active approach. Jeb's views on Cuba are well-established from his Florida governorship; we compare those views to Rand's on pp. 164-165. Jeb's views will expand to a fuller description on many political hotspots as he forms his views during 2015; but this chapter contains a comprehensive record of Jeb's views as of the end of 2014. Rand's views are clear on these three issues: stop intervening in Cuba; stop intervening with North Korea; and stop intervening with Russia.

Rand Paul on
National Security Issues

Jeb Bush on
National Security Issues

Rand Paul on Terrorism Policy

TSA is a testament to Islamic terrorist's success

The TSA is a grand testament to Islamic terrorists' success—the scene in any airport pre-9/11 versus post-9/11 is now perceived as a major victory by our enemies. We have given up so many of our liberties, all in the name of preventing another tragedy like 9/11—and that's a tragedy in itself.

There are many parts to this tragedy: great expansion of unchecked federal power; agencies 1st distorting then growing entirely beyond their mission. The combination of all of this has left us where we are today—in a mess.

First came the introduction of the "naked body" scanners, which some have accurately dubbed "porno scanners." For years, passengers on airlines, just like visitors to a secure building, have gone through metal detectors to ensure they were not carrying a weapon. In recent years government bureaucrats at the TSA decided that such measures were inadequate.

Source: Government Bullies, by Rand Paul, p.157-158, Sept. 12, 2012

TSA's primary function violates the Fourth Amendment

The TSA's primary function as an agency is to blatantly violate the Fourth Amendment, which protects Americans against unwarranted search and seizure. This agency has insulted and humiliated countless American citizens. I, along with many other travelers, do not view traveling as a crime that warrants routine government-enforced search and seizure. In fact, I view traveling as a basic right, in which Americans should be free to travel from one state to another without having to succumb to sexual harassment, public humiliation, and government theft—of both our possessions and our pride.

America is better than this.

Source: Government Bullies, by Rand Paul, p.179-180, Sept. 12, 2012

Jeb Bush on Terrorism Policy

$17M for new programs for terrorism response

Immediately following the terrorist attacks on September 11th, we acted quickly. By executive order, I put in place new programs that bolstered law enforcement's ability to deal with the terrorist threat and authorized specialized training for domestic security personnel.

I am proud of the rapid response of the Legislature in aggressively addressing this new threat. A few weeks ago, in special session, you dedicated more than $17 million in new programs to bolster homeland security, put into place harsher criminal penalties for terrorist acts, and created a new, coordinated system for law enforcement's response to terrorism.

But we must do more. I am proposing this session that we spend $45 million to further strengthen domestic security, including $6 million to continue the efforts begun in the current year.

Source: State of the State address to 2002 Florida Legislature, Jan. 22, 2002

NOTE: *The Transportation Security Administration (TSA) was created in 2001 in response to the September 11 attacks. The TSA began the airport requirements of full-body scans; body pat-downs; limiting liquids; removing shoes; and banning sharp objects in luggage. Civil libertarians claim that all of the TSA procedures invade personal privacy while adding little to actual security.*

Rand Paul on ISIL (Islamic State)

ISIS are nasty terrorists but no clear-cut American interest

Q: Do you see a clear-cut, American interest in Iraq?

PAUL: I see mostly confusion and chaos, and I think some of the chaos is created from getting involved in the Syrian civil war. You have to realize that some of the Islamic rebels that we have been supporting are actually allies of the group that is now in Iraq causing all of this trouble.

Q: ISIS, as a terrorist organization, has been billed by many as a clear and present danger. Do you see that?

PAUL: I look at it on a personal basis. I ask, "Do I want to send one of my sons, or your son, to fight to regain Mosul?" And I think, "Well ya, these are nasty terrorists, we should want to kill them." But I think, "Who should want to stop them more? Maybe the people who live there." Should not the Shiites, the Maliki government, should they not stand up? Yes, we should prevent them from exporting terror; but, I'm not so sure where the clear-cut, American interest is.

Source: Meet the Press interview, June 22, 2014

NOTE: *ISIS ("Islamic State in Iraq and Syria") began taking territory from the Iraqi government control in early 2014. The United States sent 300 "advisers" to help the Iraqi army fight ISIS, in June 2014, after ISIS had captured substantial territory.*

ISIS is more accurately known as ISIL, "Islamic State in Iraq and the Levant"; the Levant is the Eastern Mediterranean area that includes Syria, Lebanon, Israel, and Palestine.

ISIL had been fighting in Syria alongside Al-Qaeda, but broke ties with Al-Qaeda in Iraq.

Jeb Bush on ISIL (Islamic State)

ISIL's rise is because world has no clue where US will be

Jeb Bush directly blamed the rise of the Islamic State (ISIS) forces and other crises in the Middle East on a widespread lack of trust in President Barack Obama's statements. "A president's word matters," Bush said. "Language matters. The use of their bully pulpit matters. So when you say things like, 'We're gonna have a red line,' you need to mean it. You can't just say that and then say, 'Well, I was talking about the world's red line,'" Bush said, adding, "Give me a break."

Bush was referring to Obama's declaration in August 2012 that Syria's use of chemical weapons would cross "a red line for us," necessitating U.S. military intervention. Obama reneged on that commitment following Syria's apparent actual use of such weapons a year later, claiming "I didn't set a red line; the world set a red line."

"Presidents need to accept responsibility for their language," Bush said. "It needs to be taken to the bank. The problem in America today is that our friends have no clue where we will be, and so they change their behavior." By contrast, he said, "our enemies have a clue where we will be and they change their behaviors as well. And so these voids are created and bad things happen."

Source: Theodore Kettle on Newsmax.com, "Obama's Untrustworthiness Led to Rise of ISIS" Oct. 31, 2014

NOTE: *The groups fighting in the Syrian civil war can be entirely divided along Shia-Sunni lines: Assad is supported by Iran (a Shi'ite country), and by Hezbollah (a Shi'ite terrorist group); the Syrian rebels are supported by the Saudi Arabia and the Emirates (Sunni countries), and by Al-Qaeda, a Sunni terrorist group.*

That list of groups is confusing, and President Obama had trouble figuring out in June 2013 which groups to help and which to attack. Or more specifically, how to explain to Americans that we should help some groups and attack others. Obama did try to enforce the "red line," by planning aid to some groups and attacks on others, but the American public soundly rejected any support for Obama's policy, and the policy was abandoned.

Rand Paul on Benghazi

Prioritize embassy security to avoid another Benghazi

Numerous reports have documented the security failures that resulted in the tragic deaths of four Americans at the consulate in Benghazi. The failures of management that led to these decisions are reprehensible; the lapses in judgment indefensible.

One of the most troubling aspects of the Benghazi attack is the complete disregard that State Department leadership gave to the repeated requests for enhanced security. Should funding have been an issue, the State Department always has the option available to come to Congress for approval to transfer funds within accounts. No requests for reprogramming were made by the State Department.

In addition to increasing diplomatic security accounts in this budget, I have supported legislation to provide the State Department transfer authority to prioritize diplomatic security at our embassies around the world. However, it is worth noting that this money will only be effective if it is responsibly managed by officials at the State Department.

Source: A Clear Vision to Revitalize America, by Rand Paul, p. 42,
Oct. 1, 2013

Multiple requests for security at Benghazi were ignored

Q: You have blamed Republicans and Democrats, including Secretary of State Hillary Clinton, for the prosecution of foreign policy. If she's a candidate for President, is this the main argument against her candidacy?

PAUL: I think if you want to be Commander-in-Chief the bar you have to cross is will you defend the country—will you provide adequate security—and that's why Benghazi is not a political question for me. To me it's not the talking points—that's never been the most important part of Benghazi—it's the six months leading up to Benghazi where there were multiple requests for more security—and it never came. This was under Hillary Clinton's watch. She will have to overcome that—and we will make her answer for Benghazi.

Source: Meet the Press interview, June 22, 2014

Jeb Bush on Benghazi

Conflicting accounts of Benghazi emboldens terrorists

Jeb Bush said that the administration's conflicting accounts of the tragic murders of four Americans in the Benghazi terrorist attack has "emboldened" America's enemies and puts the United States "in a more perilous position." Bush added that the Obama administration's handling of the tragedy "has created a cloud that doesn't serve us well."

Bush indicated the administration's mixed messaging makes America look weak. "When the world sees us as uncertain and not surefooted, they act," he said. "Our friends act by pulling away and nervously kind of not being assured that the United States is there to support them. And our enemies are emboldened. So the tragedy of this is that four people lost their lives; great public servants. And then, because of the politics of this, the Obama administration sent such a confusing signal out that they did themselves no good," he added.

[Benghazi was] the first deadly assault on a U.S. diplomat since 1979. [It was recently revealed that] special ops soldiers made at least three requests for permission to respond to the developing firefight in Benghazi, which were denied.

Source: David Patten and Kathleen Walter, NewsMax TV, Oct. 28, 2012

NOTE: *There have been many fatal attacks on US overseas diplomatic facilities, including ambassadors killed, other than Benghazi. Following is the list of fatalities from such attacks during the George W. Bush presidency, excluding many attacks on the US Embassy in Baghdad:*
- 1/22/2002. U.S. Consulate in Calcutta, India: 5 killed.
- 6/14/2002. U.S. Consulate in Karachi, Pakistan: 12 killed.
- 2/28/2003. U.S. Embassy in Islamabad, Pakistan: 2 killed.
- 5/12/2003. U.S. Compound in Riyadh, Arabia: 36 killed (9 Americans).
- 7/30/2004. U.S. Embassy in Tashkent, Uzbekistan: 2 killed.
- 12/6/2004. U.S. Consulate in Jeddah, Saudi Arabia: 9 killed.
- 3/2/2006. U.S.Consulate Karachi,Pakistan (again):4 killed(one Diplomat).
- 9/12/2006. U.S. Embassy in Damascus, Syria: 4 killed.
- 3/18/2008. U.S. Embassy in Sana'a, Yemen: 2 killed.
- 7/9/2008. U.S. Consulate in Istanbul, Turkey: 6 killed.
- 9/17/2008. U.S. Embassy Sana'a, Yemen (again): 16 killed.

Rand Paul on September 11th

9/11 justified eliminating Taliban, but not nation-building

After Al Qaeda attacked the United States on Sept. 11, 2001, we rightly sought to bring to justice those who attacked us, to eliminate Al Qaeda's safe havens and training camps in Afghanistan, and to remove the terrorist-allied Taliban government. With hard work and sacrifice, our troops, intelligence personnel and diplomatic corps have skillfully achieved these objectives, culminating in the death of Osama bin Laden.

But over the past 10 years, our mission expanded to include a fourth goal: nation-building. That is what we are bogged down in now: a prolonged effort to create a strong central government, a national police force and an army, and civic institutions in a nation that never had any to begin with. Let's not forget that Afghanistan has been a tribal society for millenniums.

Source: Senate press release, "Let's Not Linger," July 4, 2011

Give trials to Guantanamo detainees

Q: President Obama spoke about closing Guantanamo. Do you think it should be closed?

PAUL: No. I think it's become a symbol of something though, and I think things should change. For example, I think the people being held there are bad people. What I would do though is accuse them, charge them, and try them in military tribunals, or trials. And I think that would go a long way toward showing the world that we're not going to hold them without charge forever.

Source: ABC This Week 2013 interview, May 26, 2013

NOTE: *The Taliban was the Muslim fundamentalist political party which rules most of Afghanistan. They were the largest army of the* mujaheddin, *and were funded by the CIA in the 1980s. The Taliban ruled under Shari'ah, or Islamic law as described in the Koran, which implies strict interpretation of moral codes and numerous personal restrictions.*

Jeb Bush on September 11*th*

Threat from 9/11 is unprecedented for our generation

In most years, we mark change by the passing of foreseeable events. But since I spoke here last, a new rhythm has been violently layered over the old. We awoke one morning in September, and we confronted a threat that is unprecedented for our generation.

As I have come to expect from Floridians, we have been extraordinary in our response to that threat. As a state, we will meet, and soon overcome, the obstacles that evil has devised. We will understand, and soon eliminate, any barrier that would keep this state from realizing its destiny. And when we do, we will be stronger and better for it. Floridians are united as never before, and when the current crisis has passed, we will remain bound to one another in a spirit of caring and community that will endure. Stronger, wiser, with an unshakable determination: that is the state of our state.

We must continue to thwart those who would harm us. We must renew our commitment to ensure the security of our citizens and our guests.

Source: State of the State address to Florida Legislature,
Jan. 22, 2002

NOTE: *On September 11, 2001, terrorists hijacked four commercial jets from Boston and Washington, and flew them into the World Trade Center in NYC and the Pentagon outside DC, destroying the Twin Towers and killing over 6,000 people. It was the worst terrorist incident in history.*

On September 11, 2001, Jeb Bush was serving as Governor of Florida. The State of the State speech above was his first after the terrorist attack. Jeb's brother was president of the United States at that time.

Rand Paul on Iranian Sanctions

Keep all options on the table, but don't declare war on Iran

Q: You were against the 2012 resolution saying that the US should do anything possible to prevent Iran from getting a nuclear weapon.

PAUL: I've repeatedly voted for sanctions against Iran. And I think all options should be on the table to prevent them from having nuclear weapons. I'm a stickler on what the wording is, because I don't want to have voted for something that declared war without people thinking through this. They said containment will never, ever be our policy. We woke up one day and Pakistan had nuclear weapons. If that would have been our policy towards Pakistan, we would be at war with Pakistan. The people who say, "by golly, we will never stand for that," they are voting for war.

Q: Could the US live with a nuclear armed Iran?

PAUL: It's not a good idea to announce that in advance. Should I announce to Iran, "well, we don't want you to, but we'll live with it." No, that's a dumb idea to say that you're going to live with it. However, the opposite is a dumb idea too.

Source: ABC This Week interview, April 13, 2014

NOTE: *In November 2011, the International Atomic Energy Agency (IAEA) Board of Governors criticized Iran after an IAEA report concluded that before 2003 Iran likely had undertaken research and experiments geared to developing a nuclear weapons capability. A number of Western nuclear experts have stated there was very little new in the report, that it primarily concerned Iranian activities prior to 2003.*

Iran rejected the details of the report and accused the IAEA of pro-Western bias. The IAEA Board of Governors has found Iran in non-compliance with its Nuclear Non-Proliferation Treaty safeguards agreement. Iran says its nuclear program is peaceful. Iran also claims that it was forced to resort to secrecy after US pressure caused several of its nuclear contracts with foreign governments to fall through.

Jeb Bush on Iranian Sanctions

Encourage regime change in Iran; keep military option open

Military options must be left on the table to force Iran's leaders to abandon their nuclear ambitions, according to Jeb Bush. The US should be much more assertive in encouraging regime change there as well, he said.

Bush said that not maintaining the viable prospect of US military action "empowers bad behavior in Tehran amongst its leaders." Bush criticized the Obama administration for failing to encourage internal resistance to Iran's mullahs. Iran's theocrats have subjected the "green movement" protesters to a series of brutal crackdowns.

"I think we need to be much more aggressive in supporting civil opposition to the regime in Iran," Bush said. "I was saddened to see how the Obama administration handled the post-election revolution on the streets. It seemed like we were very tepid, at a time when we should forcefully support freedom. It's part of who we are as a nation, and I think we should embrace this noble notion: If not for the United States, who? Who will be there to help?"

Source: David A. Patten and Kathleen Walter on Newsmax.com,
Nov. 29, 2010

NOTE: *Following is a list of nuclear-enabled countries as of 2015:*
- *China: 400 warheads; 45 nuclear tests*
- *France: 450 warheads; 210 nuclear tests*
- *India: Conducted tests, 1998*
- *Iran: Seeking nuclear capability*
- *Iraq: Sought nuclear capability under Saddam Hussein*
- *Israel: Unacknowledged nuclear capability*
- *North Korea: Conducted tests, 2006*
- *Pakistan: Conducted tests, 1998*
- *Russia: 23,000 warheads; 715 nuclear tests*
- *South Africa: Developed weapons but relinquished them in 1993*
- *United Kingdom: 260 warheads; 45 nuclear tests.*
- *United States: 12,000 warheads and 1,030 nuclear tests*

Rand Paul on Iraq War

Iraq War gave Iran regional hegemony and caused Mideast chaos

Q: Former Vice-President Dick Cheney said, "Too many times to count, Obama has told us he is 'ending' the war in Iraq—as though wishing makes it so." Do you agree?

PAUL: Was the war won in 2005, when many of these people said it was won? They didn't really understand the civil war that would break out. And what's going on now, I don't blame on Obama. Has he really got the solution? Maybe there is no solution. But I do blame the Iraq War on the chaos that is in the Middle East. I also blame those who are for the Iraq War for emboldening Iran. These are the same people now who are petrified of what Iran may become, and I understand some of their worry.

Q: You're not a "Dick Cheney Republican" when it comes to American power in the Middle East?

PAUL: What I would say is that the war emboldened Iran. Iran is much more of a threat because of the Iraq War than they were before-before there was a standoff between Sunnis and Shiites- now there is Iranian hegemony throughout the region.

Source: Meet the Press interview, June 22, 2014

NOTE: *Throughout most of the 1980s, Iran and Iraq fought a bloody war. It ended with no border changes, and without any US intervention.*

In 1990, Saddam Hussein invaded Kuwait, claiming it as a province of Iraq. The US and numerous allied assembled by Pres. George H. W. Bush built up a counterforce in Saudi Arabia and succeeded in 1991 in pushing Saddam's army out of Kuwait.

On the 10th anniversary of the Gulf War, President-elect George W Bush declared Iraqi leader Saddam Hussein "a big threat" and said he must be contained—by military force if necessary.

Jeb Bush on Iraq War

Keep US forces in Iraq, like we did after WWII

Bush compared keeping forces in Iraq to the post-World War II missions involving U.S. troops in Japan, Korea, and Europe, which "created a security for the world and allowed people to rise up from poverty." According to Bush, those missions "should be something that we are really proud of," and not doing something similar in Iraq "created a void that has allowed ISIS to emerge in Iraq as a force to be reckoned with."

According to Bush, "there is a consistent foreign policy for our country that has worked" since World War II under Democrats and Republicans alike, "and it starts with saying that we lead the world. We're not part of the 'community of nations,'" a term Bush said gave him nausea.

Source: Theodore Kettle on Newsmax.com, Oct. 31, 2014

Over time, people will respect our resolve in Iraq

Q: We're coming up on the ten-year anniversary of the war in Iraq which is widely seen in public opinion polls as a mistake. Do you think that will ever change?

BUSH: Yes. You know, a lot of things in history change over time. I think people will respect the resolve that my brother showed, both in defending the country and the war in Iraq. But history will judge that in a more objective way than today. The war has wound down now and it's still way too early to judge what success it had in providing some degree of stability in the region.

Source: CNN State of the Union interview, March 10, 2013

NOTE: *The Iraq War formally ended on Dec. 15, 2011. Approximately 5,000 "security contractors" will remain to guard the US Embassy in Baghdad, plus several thousand more "general support contractors." Another 9,000 US troops are just over the border in Kuwait.*

Rand Paul on Israel/Palestine

As only democracy in Mideast, Israel is important ally

Sarah Palin's endorsement [in the Kentucky GOP Senate primary] gave us a boost that energized supporters, brought in new ones, and, of course, annoyed my opponent and his Republican bosses to no end.

Palin wanted to know my position on Israel. I said that Israel was an important ally, the only democracy in the Middle East, and that I would not condemn Israel for defending herself. Later, after Palin's endorsement of me, she was grilled about it on FOX News. Of course, she defended it.

Source: The Tea Party Goes to Washington, by Rand Paul, p. 78, Feb. 22, 2011

Eventually end all foreign aid, but unrealistic for now

The issue of aid to Israel also came up last year in a meeting with the board of the Republican Jewish Coalition. Members pressed the senator, and he conceded that while he would eventually like to terminate all foreign aid, he knew that would not be realistic now. "You could see he was a work in progress," said a member of the Jewish coalition's board. "He's thinking about these issues; he's trying to learn."

Part of Paul's strategy is to appear before audiences that are not necessarily friendly to him, such as the Heritage Foundation, where he left the impression that he knew he must evolve.

Some observers say this is the evolution of a savvy politician with presidential ambitions. Paul says it is more like a slow reveal. "I've been expressing gradually where my foreign policy is," he said. "Foreign policy isn't set in stone. It isn't either-or. And it isn't always right or wrong."

Source: New York Times, May 24, 2014

Jeb Bush on Israel/Palestine

Israel will make no sacrifices when she feels threatened

Conducting the foreign policy of a great nation requires maturity and a strategic sense of America's long-term interests. With Israel, those interests lie in a firm alliance. Israel and America must work together to build a more prosperous and hopeful future for the region.

A state for the Palestinian people, side by side with Israel, will be possible only if the Palestinian people are represented by leaders committed to delivering on the promises made at the negotiating table. Ultimately, the most fruitful efforts for peace come in moments when America's word is trusted and America's commitment is certain. Anyone who claims to pursue peace in the region—especially between Israel and her neighbors—must know that Israel will make no sacrifices for peace when she feels threatened.

The future success of American foreign policy in the Middle East—and the world—will require a fresh approach. One that takes to heart the realities of the region. One that rebuilds the friendships we once enjoyed. One that reminds our enemies of our determination. And one that fundamentally believes that when America leads, the world is more stable and America's security is more certain.

Source: Jeb Bush opinion piece in National Review, March 25, 2015

NOTE: *Israel made peace with the PLO in 1993, and granted autonomy to the Palestinian Authority. That entity split in 2007 into Fatah governing the West Bank (at peace with Israel) and Hamas governing the Gaza Strip (with regular rocket fire into Israel through 2014).*

AIPAC is the American Israel Public Affairs Committee, founded in 1951. The pro-Israel group, with 100,000 grassroots members nationally, is currently considered one of the most powerful lobbying groups in Washington. Detractors claim that AIPAC support causes politicians to support Israel, as Jeb and Rand both do. Supporters claim that supporting Israel makes sense since it is the only stable democracy in the Middle East.

Rand Paul on Afghanistan War

Staying in Afghanistan will not make America safer

Last month President Obama announced plans for withdrawing by next summer the approximately 30,000 American troops sent to Afghanistan as part of the 2009 surge. We commend the president for sticking to the July date he had outlined for beginning the withdrawal. However, his plan would not remove all regular combat troops until 2014. We believe the US is capable of achieving this goal by the end of 2012. America would be more secure and stronger economically if we recognized that we have largely achieved our objectives in Afghanistan and moved aggressively to bring our troops and tax dollars home.

Sometimes our national security warrants extreme sacrifices. In this case, however, there is little reason to believe that the continuing commitment of tens of thousands of troops on a sprawling nation-building mission in Afghanistan will make America safer. Al Qaeda's presence in Afghanistan has been greatly diminished. Al Qaeda has a much larger presence in a number of other nations.

Source: Senate press release, "Let's Not Linger," July 4, 2011

NOTE: *The primary suspect of the September 11th bombings was Osama bin Laden>, an exiled Saudi millionaire based in Afghanistan. The CIA formerly funded bin Laden as a leader of the mujaheddin, or freedom fighters, when the Soviet Union occupied Afghanistan through the 1980s. Bin Laden turned against the US when troops were stationed in Saudi Arabia during the Gulf War in 1990. He issued a fatwa, or religious edict, calling for the removal of US troops from the Holy Lands of Mecca and Medina. Bin Laden's organization, al Qaeda, which means "The Base," funds terrorist training and operations, and has been implicated in past terrorist actions in the 1993 World Trade Center bombing, the 2000 USS Cole bombing, and the 1998 simultaneous attack on two US embassies in Kenya and Tanzania.*

Jeb Bush on Afghanistan War

OpEd: Not willing to distance himself from brother's Afghan policy

On five talk shows Sunday morning, Jeb Bush reminded America why he'll never be president: it's hard to distance yourself from your own last name. "I don't think there's any Bush baggage at all," the former Florida governor said on Fox News Sunday. "I love my brother. I'm proud of his accomplishments." On Meet the Press, he added that "history will be kind to George W. Bush."

To seriously challenge for the presidency, a Republican will have to pointedly distance himself from Jeb's older brother. No Republican will enjoy credibility as a deficit hawk unless he or she acknowledges that George W. Bush squandered the budget surplus he inherited. No Republican will be able to promise foreign-policy competence unless he or she acknowledges the Bush administration's disastrous mismanagement in Afghanistan and Iraq. It won't be enough for a candidate merely to keep his or her distance from W. John McCain and Mitt Romney tried that, and they failed because the Obama campaign hung Bush around their neck every chance it got. To seriously compete, the next Republican candidate for president will have to preempt that Democratic line of attack by repudiating key aspects of Bush's legacy. Jeb Bush would find that excruciatingly hard even if he wanted to. And as his interviews Sunday make clear, he doesn't event want to try.

Source: Peter Beinart in The Daily Beast, March 11, 2013

Rand Paul on Defense Spending

National defense is important, but no blank check

Q: On defense issues you're more closely associated with the left?

PAUL: I think that's an incorrect conclusion. I would say my foreign policy is right there with what came out of Ronald Reagan.

Q: But Reagan went through a huge defense buildup. One of the first things you did when you got elected was propose a nearly $50 billion cut to the Pentagon.

PAUL: Even though I believe national defense is the most important thing we do, but it isn't a blank check. Some conservatives think, oh, give them whatever they want and that everything is for our soldiers and they play up this patriotism that—oh, we don't have to control defense spending. We can't be a trillion dollars in the hole every year.

Source: ABC This Week interview, April 13, 2014

$76B in new defense spending, paid for with cuts to EPA, HUD, and foreign aid

Rand Paul is completing an about-face on a longstanding pledge to curb the growth in defense spending. Paul introduced a budget amendment calling for a nearly $190 billion infusion to the defense budget over the next two years—a roughly 16% increase.

Paul's amendment brings him in line with his likely presidential primary rivals, including Florida Sen. Marco Rubio, who introduced a measure calling for nearly the same level of increases just days ago.

The move completes a stunning reversal for Paul, who in May 2011, released his own budget that would have slashed the Pentagon, a sacred cow for many Republicans. Under Paul's original proposal, defense spending would have dropped from $553 billion in 2011 to $542 billion in 2016. But under Paul's new plan, the Pentagon will see its budget authority swell by $76 billion to $696 billion in fiscal year 2016. The boost would be offset by a $106 billion cut to funding for aid to foreign governments, climate change research and reductions to the budgets of the EPA, HUD, and the departments of Commerce and Education.

Source: Time magazine, "Defense Spending", March 27, 2015

Jeb Bush on Defense Spending

Weakness invites war: our military should equal any threat

The President's word needs to be backed by the greatest military power in the world. The president should show leadership—and commitment to solving the problem. Having a military that is equal to any threat is not only essential for the commander-in-chief—it also makes it less likely that we will need to put our men and women in uniform in harm's way. Because I believe, fundamentally, that weakness invites war—and strength encourages peace.

The threats of the 21st century will not be the same as the threats of the 20th—and it is critical that we adapt to meet this challenge. We have no reason to apologize for our leadership and our interest in serving the cause of global security, global peace and human freedom.

Source: Speech to the Chicago Council on Global Affairs, Feb. 18, 2015

Make Florida the most military-friendly state in the nation

We must protect our military bases and the $44 billion defense industry by aggressively defending our military installations in the 2005 base closure (BRAC) process. We must also find more ways to support the military men and women who serve their country from our state. I support the legislation proposed to help military families transition into our communities and our schools, as part of our effort to make Florida the most military friendly state in the nation.

Source: State of the State speech to the Florida Legislature, March 2, 2004

NOTE: President Obama proposes slowing the growth of defense spending in future years. Obama would increase the defense budget by 2% per year, while the CBO projects GDP to grow at about 3% per year. In 2017, Obama proposes $568 billion for the defense budget.

Defense spending does not include $221 billion in defense-related spending: The Department of Homeland Security's 2013 budget is $55 billion; the Department of Veterans Affairs' 2013 budget is $60 billion plus $89 billion in mandated spending; and part of the Department of Energy's 2013 budget of $35 billion goes toward maintaining our nuclear weapons.

Rand Paul on Military Priorities

We've over-militarized our foreign policy

Secretary Gates got it right when he said that we've over-militarized our foreign policy. Should we be engaged in trying to encourage stability in the world? Absolutely. But we must think before we act. Hillary's war in Libya is a prime example of acting without thinking.

Unfortunately, both parties too often seek military intervention without thinking through the possible unintended consequences. Many Republicans complain that we didn't send US ground troops or we didn't stay long enough.

The Middle East is in the midst of a 1,000-year war between Sunni and Shia—superimposed on a century-old war pitting a barbaric aberration of Islam against civilized Islam. We are foolish to believe we will solve this puzzle. We must defend vital American interests, but we must not be deluded into believing that we can remake the Middle East in an image of Western Democracy.

The civilian bureaucracy at the Pentagon has doubled in the past 30 years, gobbling up the money necessary to modernize our defense. That's why I will propose the first ever Audit of the Pentagon, and seek ways to make our defense department more modern and efficient.

Source: Tea Party response to the State of the Union address, Jan. 20, 2015

NOTE: *The 2005 BRAC report (Base Realignment and Closure Commission) recommended the following occur by 2011:*

- *9 bases for closure (originally 14 bases, but 5 later removed)*
- *13 bases for realignment*
- *12 joint bases created by merging two adjacent bases.*

Another BRAC commission is scheduled for 2015, and then every 8 years thereafter. The five bases originally slated for closure had their status reversed by political action (like Jeb describes on opposite page); the purpose of having an independent BRAC commission is to avoid such political interference.

Jeb Bush on Military Priorities

Save Florida's 21 military bases from closure or downsizing

Gov. Jeb Bush led a delegation of business and retired military leaders in meetings with top Pentagon officials and members of Florida's congressional delegation as part of a mission to save the state's military bases from possible closure or downsizing. Protecting the 21 installations and three unified commands during the 2005 Base Realignment and Closure, or BRAC, round is a one of Bush's core priorities.

Source: Bradenton (FL) Herald, Feb. 9, 2005

NOTE: *The United States Armed Forces maintain 395 military bases abroad. These bases cost billions of dollars and have not been subject to periodic BRAC-style closures since 1965. Bases by country:*

U.S. Bases in Europe		Bases in the Mideast		Bases elsewhere	
4	Bulgaria	16	Afghanistan	2	Australia
62	Germany	3	Bahrain	1	Brazil
1	Greece	1	Diego Garcia	1	Cuba
1	Greenland	1	Djibouti	2	Guam
120	Italy	2	Israel	1	Honduras
1	Kosovo	4	Kuwait	103	Japan
1	Netherlands	2	Oman	1	Singapore
1	Portugal	3	Pakistan	48	South Korea
2	Spain	1	Qatar		
1	Turkey	1	Saudi Arabia		
5	United Kingdom	3	U.A.E.		

Rand Paul on Cuba Policy

Good idea to end Cuba embargo; it hasn't worked

Paul became the first potential Republican presidential candidate to offer some support for President Barack Obama's decision to try to normalize U.S. relations with Cuba. The president's surprise announcement was slammed by several potential GOP candidates, including Jeb Bush and Marco Rubio, who said it amounted to appeasing the Castro regime.

Paul said in a radio interview that many younger Cuban Americans support opening up trade with Cuba. He also said many U.S. farmers would back Obama's moves because the country is a new market for their crops.

"The 50-year embargo just hasn't worked," Paul said. "If the goal is regime change, it sure doesn't seem to be working and probably it punishes the people more than the regime because the regime can blame the embargo for hardship. In the end, I think opening up Cuba is probably a good idea," he said. Paul's comments parallel those of Hillary Clinton.

Source: Ken Thomas on Associated Press, "Trade with Cuba,"
Dec. 18, 2014

NOTE: *President Obama said on December 17, 2014 that he would ease economic and travel restrictions on Cuba and attempt to partner with Congress to end the trade embargo. His announcement came after Cuba released American Alan Gross, who had been imprisoned for five years, and a Cuban who had spied for the U.S. In exchange, the U.S. freed three Cubans jailed in Florida. The Pope worked behind the scenes to make many of the arrangements.*

President John F. Kennedy initiated the embargo against Cuba in 1962 after Fidel Castro led the communist revolution to take over the Cuban government. As of 2015, the embargo is still in effect and is the most enduring trade embargo in modern history. Despite the existence of the embargo, the US is the fifth largest exporter to Cuba. However, Cuba must pay cash for all imports. The UN General Assembly has, since 1992, passed a resolution every year condemning the ongoing impact of the embargo and declaring it to be in violation of international law.

Jeb Bush on Cuba Policy

Strengthen the Cuban embargo instead of lifting it

Jeb Bush's call for strengthening the US embargo of Cuba signals a get-tough approach to foreign policy sure to please his political base of Cuban-American conservatives. Bush's stance sets up a clear contrast to Hillary Clinton, who wants to lift the embargo: "I would argue that instead of lifting the embargo we should consider strengthening it again to put pressure on the Cuban regime," Bush told cheering supporters at a gathering of the US Cuba Democracy PAC, a pro-embargo advocacy group.

Bush did not spell out proposals for strengthening the embargo. But he implied that he wanted to reverse travel rules made by President Obama that allow Cuban-Americans to make unlimited trips to visit relatives. "Thousands of people travel to Cuba from the US, spending billions of dollars," Bush said. "Would lifting the embargo change the fact that the government receives almost all of the money that comes from these well-intended people that travel to the island?"

Source: Sun-Sentinel, "Jeb Bush gets tough on Cuba," Dec. 3, 2014

1990: Defended anti-Castro terrorist as patriot in exile

Jeb petitioned the Justice Department in 1990 on behalf of Orlando Bosch. The anti-Castro terrorist was implicated in a car-bombing assassination and was notorious for having masterminded the bombing of a Cubana Airlines Flight in Oct. 1976, which killed all 73 on board.

At the time George H. W. Bush was CIA director. The US sanctioned terrorism against Cuba and routinely trained commandos to infiltrate the island. Jeb, who planned to run for governor of Florida, represented a rabid anti-Castro constituency, a voting bloc that held his father's anti-Castro actions at the CIA in the highest esteem. Jeb's public support for paroling Bosch further enhanced his standing in the Cuban community, which considered Bosch a patriot in exile and honored him for his murderous bombings around the globe. At this son's behest, George Bush intervened to obtain the release of the Cuban terrorist from prison and later granted Bosch US residency.

Source: The Family, by Kitty Kelley, p.407-408, Sept. 14, 2004

Rand Paul on Korea Policy

Crazy for North Korea to use force; we'd declare war

Some argue that North Korea and Iran could be emboldened if the United States elects not to use force against Assad in Syria. This is simply not true. North Korea sits atop a stockpile of weapons in close proximity to tens of thousands of US troops. If Pyongyang ever used these weapons against our troops, they would see a massive response from the US. The American people would be united, and Congress would declare war in a heartbeat. For anyone to think otherwise—be they a hawkish American pundit or a North Korean despot—is crazy.

Likewise, Iran—or any nation developing nuclear weaponry—should not doubt the military strength and unified approach of the American people toward the terrorizing of US citizens and allies. Nor should these nations doubt that international resolve will coalesce and extract harsh penalties on nations that pursue these activities. Ultimately, the US cannot and will not take any option off the table in order to protect Israel and other regional democracies.

Source: Official Senate website www.paul.senate.gov, Jan. 15, 2015

NOTE: *North Korea never signed the Nuclear Test Ban Treaty, but was criticized internationally anyway for its first nuclear test in 2006. It is estimated that North Korea possesses 10 nuclear warheads, compared to 8,500 possessed by the United States.*

As many as two million North Koreans have died from starvation since 1995. Drought and famine continue today, and South Korea is concerned that the North will attack if facing imminent political collapse.

Kim Jong-Il, the "Dear Leader" of North Korea, died in Dec. 2011, and was succeeded by his son, Kim Jong-un, now dubbed the "Great Successor." Besides his idiosyncratic personality, the new North Korean leader has been criticized for human rights violations, as well as grandstanding on nuclear weapons.

Jeb Bush on Korea Policy

South Korea success: 1952 devastation to 2014 first-world

I want to tell a story about a country that was the poorest country on the planet in 1952. The country was Korea: a country that had been ravaged by war; a country that had the highest illiteracy rate in the world; a country with no natural resources; devastated in every possible way.

Fast forward. Over 62 years, not that long in historical terms, Korea now is a first-world country. Korea has the highest literacy rate of all the countries in the world. Korean moms and dads, some of them, save everything they have, to assure that their children get tutorial help. When President Obama was in Korea a year ago, he asked, "What is the big challenge that you face in Korea today?" it's that parents want to start English in 4th grade instead of 5th grade, and it's creating enormous political pressure on the system. But If you make a command-focused commitment to education, you can change the course of a country's future.

Source: Speech at PPF 2013 Empower SC Conference, June 27, 2013

NOTE: *The 'Asian Miracle' countries are characterized by limited democracy (usually one-party) in open economies (albeit via political insiders). The 'Asian Tigers' (their alternate title) include Singapore, Hong Kong, South Korea, and Taiwan. The political relevance of each to the 2016 election is that candidates will discuss each of the Asian Tigers in the following contexts:*

- *South Korea is the capitalist contrast to communist North Korea*
- *Taiwan is the capitalist contrast to communist China*
- *Hong Kong is another capitalist contrast to communist China*
- *Singapore is the capitalist model for communist China's future*

Rand Paul on Russia Policy

Don't get stuck in Cold War idea of tweaking Russia

What Rand Paul has been saying about Russia and Ukraine is much more confusing than it is isolationist. When Moscow's pawn fled Ukraine, Sen. Paul wasn't celebrating the triumph of the Kiev democracy movement, but said, "Some on our side are so stuck in the Cold War era that they want to tweak Russia all the time and I don't think that is a good idea." Paul said he wanted "respectful" relations with Russia.

Paul's dovish line started to seem a bit embarrassing when men with unmarked uniforms began to seize control of parts of Crimea. Paul then issued this timid warning for the Kremlin: "Russia should be reminded that stability and territorial integrity go hand in hand with prosperity. Economic incentives align against Russian military involvement in Ukraine."

Eight days later, he published an essay in Time under the headline, US Must Take Strong Action Against Russian Aggression. He wrote, "It is our role as a global leader to be the strongest nation in opposing Russia's latest aggression."

Source: Forbes Magazine, March 11, 2014

NOTE: *In March 2014, Crimea held a referendum vote on whether to declare independence from Ukraine; the vote passed with 96% in favor. Russia recognized the independent Crimean Republic the next day; and the day after that, signed a treaty with Crimea's leaders annexing it to Russia. Russia then invaded and annexed the Crimea. A 1954 Soviet Decree was hence undone, which had transferred Crimea from Russia to Ukraine.*

In 2014, the eastern region of Ukraine was declared the "Donetsk People's Republic," supported by Russia but declared a terrorist group by Ukraine supporters. As of 2015, Ukraine's supporters claim that Russia supports the Donetsk group militarily, for the purpose of declaring a separate state affiliated with Russia.

Jeb Bush on Russia Policy

Passivity hasn't worked on Russia and Ukraine

Bush has joined Chris Christie and other center-right Republicans in criticizing President Obama for alleged "passivity." In a private speech in March to Sheldon Adelson and the Republican Jewish Coalition, Bush slammed Obama on Russia and Ukraine: "He was very rough on the president in terms of his handling of foreign policy, referring to the dangers of 'American passivity.'"

Back in 2012, [one pundit wrote in] Foreign Policy: "The next Republican nominee will need distance both from George W. Bush's foreign policy and from Mitt Romney's campaign. Even Jeb Bush—particularly Jeb Bush—would have to look like he was taking a very different approach to foreign policy than his brother."

But can Jeb Bush so easily make a "clean break," so to speak, with W.? According to the website On the Issues, Bush was a founding member of the Project for a New American Century, the neoconservative outfit formed in the 1990s that played a leading role in generating support for war in Iraq and whose members took up key positions in the administration of George W. Bush, Jeb's brother.

Lately, Bush hasn't said much about either PNAC, his brother or foreign policy generally. According to Defense News, Jeb Bush's views on foreign policy and defense are closer to those of his father—i.e., more centrist, more realist, more diplomacy-minded, in other words, Obama-like—than they are to the views of his militarist brother.

Chris Christie, Jeb Bush, a handful of other GOP governors: none of them have fully developed views on foreign policy.

Source: Bob and Barbara Dreyfuss, The Nation, May 30, 2014

Rand Paul vs. Jeb Bush
on International Issues

International issues focus on foreign relations and anything involving foreign nations, except the military issues covered in the previous chapter. In our national security chapter above, Jeb is just forming his views; in this chapter, that applies to the foreign relations section as well. Jeb's views are more fully formed on issues of global warming and global trade, and he has written a book on immigration issues. Rand Paul has a long voting record on all of the issues in this chapter, and are often the opposite of Jeb's views in this chapter.

The key question to be addressed by 2016: Is Jeb a neocon? That means a "neo-Conservative," the group that dominated the international policymakers of the George W. Bush administration. We conclude: No, not quite, Jeb is not a neocon like his brother George. Jeb may be advised by neocons in a third Bush Administration, but he is much more of a multilateralist, and much more cautious in his foreign policy, than the second President Bush. At issue with the George Bush presidency is that George allowed the neocons to determine policy, especially with the Iraq War (which was a major neocon goal). Jeb starts off much more knowledgeable and involved about international affairs than was George at this phase of his campaign, and although Jeb will likely have neocon advisers, Jeb does not seem as likely to follow neocon policies. On the other hand, Jeb was a founding member of Project for a New American Century (PNAC, the organization that defined the neocon movement, see p. 169). So Jeb's statements in 2015 will have to determine the answer.

The corresponding key question to be addressed in 2016 for Rand: Is he a libertarian? We address that question on pp. 232-3 (the answer is yes, Rand is a libertarian, but not as libertarian as his father Rep. Ron Paul). And also: does Rand represent the Tea Party? We address that question on pp. 211-212 (the answer is yes, Rand represents the Tea Party, but not as closely as do some of his rivals).

This chapter includes the following topics:

- *Global Warming (pp. 174-177):* including climate change and the international response. Jeb is a "skeptic" on global warming but willing to participate in global treaties if done right. Rand opposes

EPA intervention on greenhouse gases and opposes U.N. intervention on global warming.

- *Foreign Relations (pp. 178-187):* Jeb is a multilateralist who supports engaging America with the world; Rand is a non-interventionist (which he takes pains to differentiate from isolationism). Mostly Jeb defines himself as not Obama (whom he considers too passive) and not Rand Paul (whom he considers an isolationist). We attempt to define the "Rand Paul Doctrine" and the "Jeb Bush Doctrine" on pp. 184-185.

- *Global Trade (pp. 188-191):* including NAFTA (the North American Free trade Agreement) and other bilateral agreements. At issue for 2016 are expanding NAFTA to all of the Americas, and an equivalent trans-Pacific trade pact. Both Jeb and Rand are free-traders; but neither have focused much on this issue.

- *Immigration (pp. 192-199):* including border security; the border fence; and dealing with the current 12 million illegal immigrants in the US. Both Jeb and Rand support a path to citizenship, which opponents call "amnesty." Immigration, which is one of Jeb's core issues, is the most likely issue to draw an anti-immigration opponent in the Republican primary: especially the Tea Party opposes both Jeb and Rand on immigration.

Talking about immigrants means talking about Latinos: half of all immigrants today are from Latin America. And talking about immigrants means talking about the Latino vote: 70% of Latino voters supported Obama in the last election. The most important demographic is that Latinos make up 17% of the voting population now, but that will rise to 29% by 2050. Latinos support immigration reform (and in particular, amnesty) with the same lopsided support with which they support Democrats: over 70% favor amnesty. Both Jeb and Rand support outreach to Latinos on this issue, while other hard-core anti-immigration Republicans cannot make that sort of outreach.

Rand Paul on International Issues

Jeb Bush on International Issues

Rand Paul on Climate Change

Unelected EPA should not regulate greenhouse emissions

Q: Dr. Paul, you believe the government should stay out of the private sector. You said, "Get rid of regulations. Get the EPA out of our coal business down here. Get OSHA out of our small businesses." Is there no role for government in protecting our environment?

PAUL: It's a combination of federal, state and local regulations. Which way do we want to shift the debate. Do we want more federal or more local? We now have an EPA that is writing rules, saying, "If Congress doesn't pass greenhouse emissions testing, we will simply do it on our own." I think the arrogance of unelected bureaucrats to say that they create law needs to come to an end. We need to say to unelected bureaucrats, "You do not make regulations. You do not write regulations."

CONWAY: I'm against cap and trade, too. Always have been.

Source: Fox News Sunday, 2010 Kentucky Senate debate, Oct. 3, 2010

Voted YES on barring EPA from regulating greenhouse gases

Congressional Summary: To prohibit the Administrator of the Environmental Protection Agency from promulgating any regulation concerning the emission of a greenhouse gas to address climate change. The Clean Air Act is amended by adding a section entitled, "No Regulation of Emissions of Greenhouse Gases".

The definition of the term 'air pollutant' does not include a greenhouse gas, except for purposes of addressing concerns other than climate change.

Proponent's Argument for voting Yes: [Sen. McConnell, R-KY]: The White House is trying to impose a backdoor national energy tax through the EPA. It is a strange way to respond to rising gas prices. But it is perfectly consistent with the current Energy Secretary's previously stated desire to get gas prices in the US up to where they are in Europe.

Source: Vast Right-Wing Conspiracy, by A. Carpenter, p. 62-63, Oct. 11, 2006

Jeb Bush on Climate Change

I'm a skeptic about global warming

Q: Do you believe global warming is primarily man-made?

A: I'm a skeptic. I'm not a scientist. I think the science has been politicized. I would be very wary of hollowing out our industrial base even further. It may be only partially man-made. It may not be warming; the last six years we've actually had mean temperatures that are cooler. I think we need to be very cautious before we dramatically alter who we are as a nation because of it.

Source: Tucker Carlson interview of Jeb Bush in Esquire, Aug. 1, 2009

A "patriotic energy policy" will yield far more revenue

What I would do is advocate policies that would create high growth because the revenue collected by government when you're growing at 3.5% instead of 1.5% is exponentially more. And high growth over a sustained period of time by having a patriotic energy policy, bringing regulation to the 21st Century, immigration reform would be a good one, reforming our education system, tax policy – all those things would yield, I think, far more revenue. That should be where there's the common ground. And in return, there should be some give and take as it relates to entitlement reform. You could get to a place where our fiscal house would be in order if we achieved that. The president has not been willing to discuss that but in the last week, he's begun to at least reach out to Republicans which is quite encouraging.

Source: CBS Face the Nation, March 10, 2013

Rand Paul on Kyoto Treaty

Cap-and-trade has no impact on global temperatures

Paul signed the *Contract From America* [which includes]:

- *Reject Cap & Trade:*
- Stop costly new regulations that would increase unemployment, raise consumer prices, and weaken the nation's global competitiveness with virtually no impact on global temperatures.
- Explore proven energy reserves & keep energy prices low.

Source: The Contract From America, on Jul 8, 2010

NOTE: Cap-and-Trade refers to a carbon dioxide (CO_2) emissions policy where the amount of CO_2 is "capped" at a government-specified emission amount, and then the right to emit CO_2 is "traded" via emission permits. The result would be instituting a new fee for emitting carbon dioxide and other greenhouse gases. A similar program was used successfully to battle acid rain via sulfur dioxide emission permits trading on the Chicago Mercantile Exchange.

Jeb Bush on Kyoto Treaty

Kyoto Treaty must include reductions by all countries

Bush adopted the National Governors Association policy: The Governors recommend that the federal government continue to seek the advice of state and local officials with expertise in economic, trade, jobs, public health, and environmental issues and assess the potential economic and environmental consequences of proposed policies and measures, including a thorough and broadly accepted analysis of costs and benefits. The Governors recommend that the US:

- not sign or ratify any agreement that mandates new commitments to limit or reduce greenhouse gas emissions for the US, unless such an agreement mandates new specific scheduled commitments to limit or reduce greenhouse gas emissions for developing countries within the same compliance period;

- aggressively undertake strategies for including emissions-reduction commitments from developing countries;

- not sign or ratify any agreement that would result in serious harm to the US economy;

- support flexible policies and measures in continuing negotiations that provide an opportunity for the US to meet global environmental goals without jeopardizing US jobs, trade, or economic competitiveness; and

- ensure that no single sector, state, or nation is disproportionately disadvantaged by the implementation of international policies.

Source: NGA policy NR-11, Climate Change International Policy on Aug 15, 2000

NOTE: *"Kyoto" refers to a Climate Change Treaty which sets carbon dioxide reduction targets for the US and other developed countries, via a policy that has become known as "cap-and-trade." Completed in 1998, the US has not yet signed. This is politically controversial because it would require the US to cut CO_2 emissions, which is potentially costly. "Cap-and-trade" is intended to minimize the cost, but has become a buzzword for the opposition.*

Rand Paul on International Treaties

Oppose the United Nations' Arms Trade Treaty

Paul signed Letter to President Obama from 50 Senators:

We write to express our concern and regret at your decision to sign the United Nations' Arms Trade Treaty. For the following reasons, we cannot give our advice and consent to this treaty:

- The treaty includes only a weak, non-binding reference to the lawful ownership and use of firearms, and recognizes none of these activities, much less individual self-defense, as fundamental individual rights. It encourages governments to collect the identities of individual end users of imported firearms at the national level, which would constitute the core of a national gun registry

- The State Department has acknowledged that the treaty is "ambiguous." By becoming party to the treaty, the US would therefore be accepting commitments that are inherently unclear.

- The criteria at the heart of the treaty are vague and easily politicized. They will steadily subject the US to the influence of internationally-defined norms, a process that would impinge on our national sovereignty.

- The treaty criteria as established could hinder the US in fulfilling its strategic, legal, and moral commitments to provide arms to key allies such as Taiwan and Israel.

We urge you to notify the treaty depository that the US does not intend to ratify the Arms Trade Treaty, and is therefore not bound by its obligations. As members of the Senate, we pledge to oppose the ratification of this treaty, and we give notice that we do not regard the US as bound to uphold its object and purpose.

Source: Letter to Obama from 50 Senators on Sep 25, 2013

Jeb Bush on International Treaties

We are leader among equals in community of nations

Bush said relatively little about his brother or his father in [his foreign policy speech to the U.S.-Cuba Democracy PAC]. He spent far more time talking about President Obama. Bush said the current president violated his first foreign-policy precept: to lead both the United States and the world. "We are not an equal partner in this so-called community of nations. We are a leader among equals," Bush said. "First, I think the United States needs to lead. Lead with humility. Lead with respect. But lead."

In calling for a foreign policy laced with "humility," Bush echoed his brother's call in 2000 to have a "humble" foreign policy. A year later, the US became far more interventionist after the 9/11 attacks, which ultimately helped lead the nation into invading Afghanistan and Iraq.

One of Bush's precepts was more of a slogan: "Words matter." He said that time and again, Obama has made threats or promises and then failed to act: "Presidents need to set United States aspirations and intentions where there is little gap between words and deeds," Bush said. "Think of the 'Russian reset.' Think of the 'Syrian red line.' Think of the 'pivot to Asia.' Think of taking out ISIS."

Bush said Obama failed to accomplish any of these goals: "It undermines our credibility in the world. Our allies don't trust us. And our enemies don't fear us. There is no situation worse for stability and peace than that," Bush said. "The iron rule of superpower deterrent is 'mean it when you say it.' And it has been broken by this president."

Source: Miami Herald, "The 'Jeb Bush Doctrine' makes debut,"
Dec. 2, 2014

Rand Paul on American Exceptionalism

America's exceptionalism is notion that all should be free

The state of our economy is tenuous but our people remain the greatest example of freedom and prosperity the world has ever known.

People say America is exceptional. I agree, but it's not the complexion of our skin or the twists in our DNA that make us unique. America is exceptional because we were founded upon the notion that everyone should be free to pursue life, liberty, and happiness.

For the first time in history, men and women were guaranteed a chance to succeed based *NOT* on who your parents were but on your own initiative and desire to work. We are in danger, though, of forgetting what made us great.

Source: Tea Party Response to State of the Union Address, Feb. 12, 2013

Jeb Bush on American Exceptionalism

God grants liberty only to ready to defend it

Last month, we welcomed home almost 2,000 soldiers of the Florida National Guard from the war on terror. Some won't make it home. It has been said, "God grants liberty only to those who love it and are always ready to defend it." Because of the thousands who continue the fight, America will always be free.

We must acknowledge the great debt we owe patriots like [our lost soldiers]. We should honor their service by ensuring that our actions, both in and out of this chamber, are worthy of their sacrifice. We must serve this state as honorably and effectively as they serve this country. I believe we are on the right path.

Source: State of the State speech to the Florida Legislature,
March 2, 2004

NOTE: *"American exceptionalism" means that America has a unique status in the world today. The interest in American exceptionalism counters Obama's rejection of the concept, when Obama said, "Sure, I believe in American exceptionalism in the same way the British believe in British exceptionalism." Republicans generally interpret that as meaning, "No, I don't believe in your version of American exceptionalism at all." Jeb has avoided the phrase "American exceptionalism," while Rand embraces it (without the militarism that often accompanies it).*

Rand Paul on International Alliances

Stop sending foreign aid to people who don't like us

We continue sending billions to Afghanistan, yet Afghan president Hamid Karzai says that if neighboring Pakistan and the US went to war, his country would side with Pakistan. Pakistani leaders have made similar comments, that if the US goes to war with Iran, Pakistan will side with Iran. Yet we continue to send Afghanistan and Pakistan billions of US taxpayer dollars. Why?

We cannot continue to try to bully allies or pay off our enemies. So many of the countries we send aid to dislike us, regularly disrespect us, and openly tell the world they will side with our enemies.

America doesn't even have the money to send them. We're borrowing the money from China to aid people who don't like us. This is illogical. It's an insult. And it should end.

Source: Government Bullies, by Rand Paul, p.199, Sept. 12, 2012

Exit the UN; maintain US sovereignty

Q: Do you support US withdrawal from the United Nations?

A: Yes.

Q: Would you forbid US troops from serving under UN command?

A: Yes.

Q: Will you restrict the Executive's ability to forge international agreements that lessen our sovereignty?

A: Yes.

Reference: Campaign for Liberty survey of 2010 Congressional candidates, Nov. 1, 2010

NOTE (opposite page): *NATO, the North Atlantic Treaty Organization was, during the Cold War, the main counterbalance to the Soviet Union. Now it includes 28 countries, including some of the former Soviet bloc. At issue in 2015 is which former Soviet allies to include in NATO: the most recent additions were Albania and Croatia in 2009.*

Jeb Bush on International Alliances

Nourish our existing alliances: that means NATO & Israel

Bush outlined a series of principles as necessary for an effective U.S. foreign policy: "The appropriate traditional foreign policy," Bush said, "requires you to nourish the alliances that exist in the world and have kept us safe. That means NATO. That means our relationship with Israel. These alliances have been built by American leadership and we need to nourish them so that they're real rather than just paper tigers."

Bush also blamed Obama for "gutting the military and our intelligence capabilities in a world where these asymmetric threats are real." Bush concluded that "in every one of those 4 or 5 principles of foreign policy I would say that the president's let us down." Bush explained Obama's failures: "you need to lead, and reacting is not leadership."

Source: Theodore Kettle on Newsmax.com, "Obama's Untrustworthiness Led to Rise of ISIS" Oct. 31, 2014

US should shape events and build alliances of free people

My goal today is to explore how America can regain its leadership in the world. And why that leadership is more necessary than ever. American leadership projected consistently and grounded in principle has been a benefit to the world.

I have doubts whether this administration believes American power is such a force. Under this administration, we are inconsistent and indecisive. We have lost the trust & the confidence of our friends. We definitely no longer inspire fear in our enemies.

The great irony of the Obama Presidency is this: Someone who came to office promising greater engagement with the world has left America less influential in the world.

The United States has an undiminished ability to shape events and build alliances of free people. We can project power and enforce peaceful stability in far-off areas of the globe. To do so, I believe we need to root our foreign policy in a set of priorities and principles.

Source: Speech at Chicago Council on Global Affairs, Feb. 18, 2015

Rand Paul on Foreign Policy Doctrine

My worldview: engage both friend and foe in dialogue

People sometimes ask me what my worldview is. I really am a believer that foreign policy must be viewed by events as they present themselves, not as we wish them to be. The world of foreign policy has been turned on its head in the past decade.

I believe the answers to most problems that confront us around the world can and should be approached by engaging both friend and foe in dialogue. No, I don't naively think that dialogue always works, but I believe we should avoid the rigidity of saying that dialogue never works. I believe we should approach diplomacy from the notion that dialogue is nearly always preferable to war but that potential enemies should never mistake, as Reagan put it, our reluctance for war, with a lack of resolve.

I consider foreign policy to be an unending process of learning and that I am very open to learning new ideas, whether they are indeed new, or maybe just new to me.

Source: Rand Paul OpEd in The National Interest, Jan. 16, 2014

No isolationism; but don't go abroad seeking enemies

America's national security mandate shouldn't be one that reflects isolationism, but instead one that is not rash or reckless, a foreign policy that is reluctant, restrained by Constitutional checks and balances but does not appease; this balance should heed the advice of America's sixth president, John Quincy Adams, who advised, "America goes not abroad in search of monsters to destroy. She is the well-wisher to freedom and independence of all."

Source: Vision to Revitalize America, by Rand Paul, p. 37, Oct. 1, 2013

NOTE: *What would the "Rand Paul Doctrine" be? Even at this early stage, it is pretty clear: Rand believes in a foreign policy of non-intervention along the lines of President George Washington's warning against "foreign entanglements." Rand differentiates that from isolation-ism because he believes in engaging governments abroad in dialog, but not in war. This was once a well-established policy in American history, but not since President Teddy Roosevelt.*

Jeb Bush on Foreign Policy Doctrine

Neo-isolationism and American passivity both have dangers

Jeb Bush attacked the White House's approach to foreign policy in a speech given to the Republican Jewish Coalition. Bush focused on economic policy in his remarks but also impressed the pro-Israel group with his defense of muscular American foreign policy.

"He showed a lot of knowledge about foreign policy that he must have been working hard to acquire," said Ari Fleischer, the former White House Press Secretary and a board member of the RJC, noting Bush discussed diplomatic challenges presented by countries like Ukraine, Russia and Moldova. "He was very rough on the president in terms of his handling of foreign policy, referring to the dangers of 'American passivity.'"

The son and brother of presidents, Bush cautioned the Republican party against "neo-isolationism," a line universally understood as a shot at Rand Paul. Bush also pushed back on Democratic attacks that whenever a Republican calls for a more activist foreign policy that they are "warmongering."

Source: Time Magazine, "American Passivity," March 28, 2014

NOTE: *The "Bush Doctrine" from the George W. Bush presidency is usually defined as taking a hard line against terrorism and defending American interests abroad, and doing both pre-emptively.*

What will the "Jeb Doctrine" be? At this stage, Jeb focuses on differentiating himself. Certainly he recognizes a more multi-polar world than a bipolar world (like during his father's presidency). The excerpt above, which we posit as a first pass of a "Jeb Doctrine," differentiates Jeb from Obama's "passivity" and from Sen. Rand Paul's "neo-isolationism."

Jeb's focus on immigration policy and on free trade perhaps indicates that his focus would be on the Americas, but we cite his comments on China, Israel, and NATO elsewhere in this chapter. Mostly, it's too early to define a "Jeb Doctrine," other than what it is not.

Rand Paul on Ebola Policy

Temporary stop on elective travel to fight Ebola

Q: Is the government following the right policies on Ebola?

PAUL: I think the president's biggest mistake was saying, "oh, it's no big deal, you can't catch it if you're sitting on a bus. And we're not going to stop any travel." It's very contagious when someone is sick. I don't think anybody should be riding on a bus or coming from Liberia to visit when they could be contagious. So, I think a temporary stop of travel for elective travel, if you're coming to visit your relatives, couldn't that wait for a few months?

Q: Do you think we ought to tighten the restrictions on who can come to this country?

PAUL: From the beginning of our country, we always had restrictions on infectious disease. That was one of the primary things we did at our border. Commercial travel for people who just want to visit the US, that really isn't a necessity, and we can wait few months on it. And it would make our problem a lot less if we were only thinking about health care workers coming back.

Source: Face the Nation 2014 interview, Nov. 2, 2014

NOTE: *The largest Ebola outbreak in history began in West Africa in December 2013. The disease was first identified in 1976, but the 2014 outbreak was the first to infect cities rather than rural areas. After one year, about 6,000 people have died from 17,000 cases, mostly in Guinea, Sierra Leone, and Liberia.*

Unlike most viruses, Ebola is infectious even after its host has died; hence many people get infected while preparing the dead for burial (until special Ebola-safe burial practices took effect). At greatest risk are the doctors and nurses treating the ill, since the virus spreads though contact with bodily fluids, which are commonly exposed during treatment.

President Obama's response has been to send U.S. military personnel to assist with constructing more hospital beds and other needed infrastructure. The medical infrastructure of the affected countries has been severely damaged, with the deaths of many doctors and nurses.

Jeb Bush on Ebola Policy

Handle Ebola crisis like I handled anthrax in Florida

Former Florida Gov. Jeb Bush criticized President Barack Obama's initial handling of the Ebola crisis as "incompetent," saying it gave rise to unneeded fears among the American public about the virus. Bush also said in a wide-ranging discussion at Vanderbilt University that he supports travel restrictions for people who have been to the most severely affected countries in Africa.

Bush said Obama should have been more "clear and concise" about his plans, and lent more credibility to health officials leading the response. "It looked very incompetent to begin with, and that fueled fears that may not be justified," Bush said. "And now you have states that are legitimately acting on their concerns, creating a lot more confusion than is necessary."

Bush contrasted what he characterized as the president's indecisive approach on Ebola to his own actions as governor when anthrax was mailed to a supermarket tabloid in Florida after the 9/11 terrorist attacks in 2001. "We gave people a sense of calm, what the plan was," Bush said. "We talked in plainspoken English. We were totally engaged."

Source: Erik Schelzig on Associated Press, Oct. 28, 2014

NOTE: *President Obama has stated that he will not impose travel restrictions on West Africa, an action which has been demanded by many Americans, except to screen incoming air passengers. Obama states that restricting air travel would hinder the medical response because fewer doctors and nurses could fly into the affected area. Rand and Jeb both disagree.*

Rand Paul on China Policy

China trade improves economy *AND* makes fight less likely

When I was about ten years old, like many conservative middle-class families, our inclination was to resist anything to do with Red China. In that black and white world, you were either for us or against us. Trade with China was thought to be trade with the enemy. A funny thing happened, though, along the way. Many conservatives came to understand a larger truth. As trade began to blossom with China, many conservatives, myself included, came to admit that trade improves our economic well-being *AND* makes us less likely to fight. The success of trade with China made many conservatives rethink their view of the world.

People sometimes ask me what my worldview is. My response is that even if you've crisscrossed the globe, I'm not sure that the world doesn't change by the time you return to the same spot twice. I really am a believer that foreign policy must be viewed by events as they present themselves, not as we wish them to be.

Source: Rand Paul OpEd in The National Interest, Jan. 16, 2014

NOTE: *China, the world's largest Communist country, will soon become the world's largest economy (estimated to pass the U.S. in 2024). In 2014, China's economy grew at an annual rate of 7.4%, despite the lingering Great Recession (which only slowed China's growth slightly). U.S. trade with China totaled $562 billion in 2013, but with a $319 billion trade deficit. The U.S. has issues with China on currency manipulation, export dumping, and labor conditions within China. Those trade-related issues will dominate U.S.-China relations in the 2016 campaign and afterwards.*

Jeb Bush on China Policy

Supports economic cooperation between US and China

Chinese Vice President Xi Jinping met with former Governor of Florida Jeb Bush Tuesday at the Great Hall of the People in Beijing, calling for closer cooperation between China and the United States.

For his part, Bush said that he will continue making contributions to the development of bilateral ties and economic cooperation between the two nations.

Source: Xinhua News (China), "Xi meets Jeb Bush," Jan. 17, 2012

Four visits to Taiwan to increase trade exchange

Vice President Annette Lu asked Florida Governor Jeb Bush, brother of US President George W. Bush, to convey greetings to the US president. Lu, who sat beside the governor at a national banquet given by El Salvador's new President, asked the governor to convey her appreciation to the US leader for his long-term support for Taiwan.

Knowing of Jeb Bush's friendship with Therese Shaheen, the former chairperson of the American Institute in Taiwan, Lu also asked him to convey her greetings to Shaheen. They also talked about increasing trade exchanges between Taiwan and Florida. The governor said that he has visited Taiwan four times, with the last visit in 1991. Lu invited him to visit again, and he said he would consider this. In turn, the governor invited Lu to visit his state.

Source: Xinhua Taipei Times(Taiwan), page 5, June 3, 2004

NOTE: The US, the ROC, and the PRC agreed in 1972 to the 'One China' policy, under which all parties abide by the fiction that China is one country currently under two governments but awaiting eventual reunification. China is formally known as 'the People's Republic of China', or 'PRC.' The PRC has been ruled by the Chinese Communist Party since 1949. Taiwan is known as 'the Republic of China' or 'rOC.' Taiwan is an island off the coast of the PRC, and has a democratically elected government. Taiwan split from the PRC during the Communist Revolution, when the former government was driven off the mainland by the Communists.

Rand Paul on Free Trade

Accompany free trade laws with other export inducers

Over the past several years, the President has taken the laudable step of urging Congress to pass free trade laws in order to elevate exports. However, apart from the effort to encourage free trade, the President's efforts to create an environment conducive to competing in a global economy have been largely misguided. The President and the central bank have attempted to increase exports by destroying the value of the dollar here at home.

The President's agenda of increasing taxes on top of a weak dollar policy is inhibiting the country's ability of to compete overseas. One of the fundamental keys to export growth is investment. The correlation between tax rates, investment and export is demonstrated by the tremendous export opportunities and growth of East Asia.

Tax rates affect the investment decisions of firms and individuals by altering the cash flow of investment opportunities, and decrease the return on investment, resulting in overall reduced investment.

Source: A Clear Vision to Revitalize America, by Rand Paul, p. 17-8, Oct 1, 2013

__NOTE:__ 'Globalization' refers generally to free trade, open borders, improved communication and transportation, and the commerce implications of the Internet. Specifically, anti-globalization advocates refer to the negative aspects of free trade on environmental and labor standards. At issue is that open borders cause corporations to seek out the lowest environmental and labor standards to minimize production costs, thereby pressuring for lower standards globally. The opposite of 'globalization' is 'fair trade,' meaning placing restrictions on imports based on environmental, labor, or other concerns. Supporting fair trade implies the speaker is against free trade; Jeb and Rand are both free-traders who support globalization.

Jeb Bush on Free Trade

Advocated Miami as HQ for Free Trade Area of the Americas

An international summit this month could move the Western Hemisphere toward becoming a free trade zone. Florida expects to be at the heart of the Free Trade Area of the Americas, the proposed $13 trillion market that would serve 800 million consumers in 34 countries. Local business leaders, backed by Gov. Jeb Bush, want Miami to become home to the FTAA's headquarters and reap the benefits of enhanced trade and commerce. But Florida's sugar and citrus growers fear the trade talks could lead to the elimination of tariffs, opening them up to competition from cheaper produce from Brazil and potentially dooming their industries.

Jeb Bush has aggressively courted support for the headquarters. The governor says his brother's decision on backing a U.S. city for the headquarters—either Atlanta or Miami—"will be based on the merits of the location." The eventual winner must be approved by the 34 nations that comprise the trade group.

Source: 7 News WSVN coverage of FTAA, Nov. 12, 2003

NOTE: *The Trans-Pacific Partnership is a proposed free trade agreement between the U.S. and Australia, Brunei, Canada, Chile, Japan, Malaysia, Mexico, New Zealand, Peru, Singapore, and Vietnam. Negotiations began in 2005; China, Mexico, and South Korea may also join.*

The TPP is potentially the largest free trade agreement in the world, laying the framework for a "free trade area of the Pacific," analogous to the "free trade area of the Americas" (FTAA). Negotiations have been mostly held in secret, a source of some controversy. Other controversial topics include trade barriers and currency manipulation (by the Asian nations) and labor and environmental issues (by China).

The FTAA is an extension of NAFTA to include the entire North American continent; negotiations began in 2001. It was scheduled to take effect by 2005, but has been met by strong anti-corporate protests.

Rand Paul on Latin American Policy

Volunteer eye surgery for blind kids in Guatemala

In a makeshift operating room in remote Guatemala, a side of Senator Rand Paul most people have never seen: The eye surgeon, on a mission to help the blind and near-blind see in a country where more than half the population lives in poverty. He's one of 28 American volunteers organized by the Moran Eye Center in Utah.

Rand Paul says, "This is an amazing enterprise. We have a surgery center. We have a dental clinic and we have a place doing glasses."

Scores of people line up every day for a week—hoping American doctors can give them their sight—and their lives back. A 79 year-old great-grandmother who has cataracts. A farmer just wants to see again so he can work in his field. A mission to restore sight, and hope, to the poorest of the poor.

When asked if this helps his presidential ambitions, Paul notes, "I've been doing this kinda stuff for 20 years—I think the first kids I operated on were 1996. This isn't something new that we're doing. A physician is who I am."

Source: Meet the Press interview, Aug. 24, 2014

NOTE: *President Hugo Chavez of Venezuela (cited on opposite page) was a nationalist and a Marxist. Because of his connection to Communism, he was considered an enemy of America; but because of Venezuela's oil wealth and drug pipeline, Venezuela was important for American policy. In 2006, President Chavez spoke at the United Nations the day after President George W. Bush had spoken there, and said, "Yesterday, the devil came here. And it smells of sulfur still today. From this rostrum, the president of the United States, the gentleman to whom I refer as the devil, came here, talking as if he owned the world. Truly. As the owner of the world." Chavez died in office in 2013; relations have still not thawed.*

Jeb Bush on Latin American Policy

Deploy military on both sides of the US-Mexican border

Fighting the drug cartels at the border may present a threat of potentially epic proportions, calling for a strong response. The cartels are paramilitary organizations with dangerous and sophisticated weaponry. Our Border Patrol officers are neither trained nor equipped to blunt the cartels' firepower if it comes to that. As a result, the president should be authorized to deploy military or National Guard forces if necessary to counter the cartels' threat and secure the US border.

Preferable to US military deployment would be efforts to increase the effectiveness of Mexican authorities in dealing with the cartels on their side of the border. US officials have worked closely with their Mexican counterparts, including the deployment of unmanned aerial surveillance vehicles and the opening of a compound to gather intelligence in northern Mexico.

Source: Immigration Wars, by Jeb Bush, p. 53, March 5, 2013

2010: Ineptitude will bring down Chavez regime in Venezuela

Bush has appeared particularly unwilling to push back against the neoconservatives who supported his brother's administration, at times echoing their complaints about the Obama administration's foreign policy.

Bush mused that "sheer ineptitude and incompetency and corruption will bring down the [Hugo] Chavez regime" in Venezuela, "but we can't sit back passively and let this happen naturally." Instead, Bush advocated offering U.S. support to "elements of Venezuelan society that are fighting back against" the democratically elected Chavez, who eventually died of cancer in early 2013 after being resoundingly reelected.

Source: International Relations Center "RightWeb" on Jeb Bush, April 1, 2014

Rand Paul on Path to Citizenship

Illegals are not bad people, but we have to control border

Q: Jeb Bush talked about how we shouldn't let the immigration issue rile people up, saying, "Yes, they broke the law, but it's not a felony. It's an act of love." Do you agree with him on this?

PAUL: You know, I think he might have been more artful, maybe, in the way he presented this. But I would have said is, people who seek the American dream are not bad people.

Q: Even if they came into this country illegally?

PAUL: They are not bad people. However, we can't invite the whole world. When you say they're doing an act of love and you don't follow it up with, "but we have to control the border," people think well because they're doing this for kind reasons that the whole world can come to our country.

Source: ABC This Week interview, April 13, 2014

Replace de facto amnesty with bipartisan reform

Paul would aim to secure the border before illegal immigrants could begin taking steps toward citizenship, as a necessary first step to get support from conservatives. Congress would also have to agree annually for 5 years that border security was progressing in order for the other reforms to keep moving forward. In year two of his plan, illegal immigrants would begin to be issued temporary work visas, and would have to wait in line behind those already in the system before moving forward toward citizenship. A bipartisan panel would determine the number of visas per year. High-tech visas would be expanded and a special visa for entrepreneurs would be issued.

Paul would not attempt to crack down on employers by expanding working verification systems, something he says is tantamount to "forcing businesses to become policemen."

"My plan will not grant amnesty or move anyone to the front of the line," Paul says. "But what we have now is de facto amnesty."

Source: Associated Press in Los Angeles Times, March 18, 2013

Jeb Bush on Path to Citizenship

There is no realistic pathway to citizenship for most people

Of the many serious and legitimate criticisms that can be leveled against our current immigration system, two in particular stand out in terms of hugely detrimental impact:

- We are not bringing in highly skilled immigrants in sufficient numbers to meet our needs and to maximize future American prosperity.

- There is no realistic pathway for most people who simply wish to become American citizens.

There is a single major explanation for both problems: our immigration policy is driven by an overriding preference for family reunification, which in turn is very broadly defined.

Source: Immigration Wars, by Jeb Bush, p. 17-19, March 5, 2013

Path to legal resident status: pay fines & no criminals

It is in no one's interest for illegal immigrants and their families to live in the shadows. We need everyone to participate in the mainstream economy, to pay taxes, to participate openly in their communities, to be willing to report crimes—that is to say, to be accountable, responsible members of society. That cannot occur when people fear they will be arrested if their immigration status is known.

We propose a path to permanent legal resident status for those who entered our country illegally as adults and who have committed no additional crimes of significance. The first step in obtaining that status would be to plead guilty to having committed the crime of illegal entry, and to receive an appropriate punishment consisting of fines and/or community service. Anyone who does not come forward under this process will be subject to automatic deportation, unless they choose to return voluntarily to their native countries.

Source: Immigration Wars, by Jeb Bush, p. 42-43, March 5, 2013

Rand Paul on Sources of Immigration

See immigrants as assets, not liabilities

We are the party that embraces hard work and ingenuity, therefore we must be the party that embraces the immigrant who wants to come to America for a better future. We must be the party who sees immigrants as assets, not liabilities. We must be the party that says, "If you want to work, if you want to become an American, we welcome you."

Source: Tea Party Response to State of the Union Address, Feb. 12, 2013

We will find a place for illegal immigrants in America

Republican Sen. Rand Paul of Kentucky is endorsing a pathway to citizenship for the nation's 11 million illegal immigrants. In a speech, the potential 2016 presidential candidate declares, "If you wish to live and work in America, then we will find a place for you."

Paul's path to citizenship would come with conditions that could make it long and difficult for illegal immigrants. Chief among these, Congress would have to agree first that progress was being made on border security.

Paul's speech is peppered with Spanish phrases from his youth in Texas, references to his immigrant grandparents and praise for Latino culture. He says his party must adopt a new face toward Hispanics and says conservatives must be part of it. "Immigration reform will not occur until conservative Republicans, like myself, become part of the solution. I am here today to begin that conversation," Paul says. "Let's start that conversation by acknowledging we aren't going to deport" the millions already here, he says.

Source: Associated Press in Los Angeles Times, March 18, 2013

Jeb Bush on Sources of Immigration

Immigration is 'not a felony' but 'an act of love'

Jeb Bush said the debate over immigration reform needs to move past derisive rhetoric describing illegal immigrants. The former Florida governor said that people who come to the US illegally are often looking for opportunities to provide for their families that are not available in their home countries.

"Yes, they broke the law, but it's not a felony. It's an act of love, it's an act of commitment to your family," Bush said. "I honestly think that is a different kind of crime, that there should be a price paid, but it shouldn't rile people up that people are actually coming to this country to provide for their families," he said.

"I think we need to kind of get beyond the harsh political rhetoric to a better place." Bush acknowledged that his comments would be recorded. "So be it," he said before discussing immigration reform, an area where he splits from many in the Republican Party in lobbying for a comprehensive overhaul.

Source: Dana Davidsen on CNN Politicker, "Act of love," April 7, 2014

Immigrants are committed to family, even if illegally here

"Immigrants create far more businesses than native-born Americans, over the last 20 years," Jeb said at the Faith and Freedom Coalition Conference in June 2013. "Immigrants are more fertile, and they love families, and they have more intact families, and they bring a younger population. Immigrants create an engine of economic prosperity."

Source: Ben Smith on BuzzFeed.com, "Terrible Candidate," April 7, 2014

Rand Paul on Comprehensive Immigration Reform

Status quo is untenable; we must do some sort of reform

Q: On the issue of immigration—is a path to citizenship something that the Republican Party needs to rethink its opposition to?

PAUL: I think that everyone needs to be for some form of immigration reform because the status quo is untenable. I think that if we do nothing, 11 million more people may be coming illegally, so we have to do something. I am for immigration reform, but I insist that you secure the border first because if you have a beacon, of some kind of forgiveness, without a secure border, the whole world will come.

Q: Does a "pathway to citizenship" mean amnesty in your book?

PAUL: I think that that's the whole point: What is amnesty? Because, [for those who say] "no deportation and no amnesty," well, if you're not going to deport people you are somehow changing the current law because the current law says everybody must go.

Q: But you've said that the party should give up this word "amnesty"?

PAUL: I think we need to get beyond it. We need some form of immigration reform.

Q: And a path to citizenship?

PAUL: Well, the path to citizenship is a longer, more difficult goal.

Q: But you don't rule it out as an end game?

PAUL: What I would say is that at this point in time I don't think any type of immigration reform will get out of Washington that includes a path to citizenship. But I do think that there is a path to a secure border and an expanded work visa program.

Source: Meet the Press 2014 interview, June 22, 2014

NOTE: "Comprehensive reform" is a politicized buzzword that means "provide amnesty and citizenship benefits for illegal immigrants already here, while securing the border and prosecuting illegal employers against new illegal immigration." Opponents of comprehensive reform would prefer a piecemeal approach: their buzzword is "secure the border first," before dealing with any benefits or any other issues.

Jeb Bush on Comprehensive Immigration Reform

6-part proposal for comprehensive immigration reform

1. *Fundamental Reform:* Comprehensive interrelated approach because system is broken, and to achieve bipartisan consensus.

2. *A Demand-Driven Immigration System:* Replace overriding preference for family reunification with work-based immigration.

3. *An Increased Role for the States:* Share federal authority over immigration policy [such as] social services and providing benefits.

4. *Dealing With Current Illegal Immigrants:* We propose a path to permanent legal resident status for those who plead guilty to having entered our country illegally as adults and who have committed no additional crimes of significance.

5. *Border Security:* Broader immigration reform is an essential component of border security; we can't do one without the other.

6. *Toward a More Vibrant Future:* Getting immigration policy right will allow us to reclaim the prosperity that in recent years has eluded our grasp.

Source: Immigration Wars, by Jeb Bush, p. 12-62, March 5, 2013

Reform must make it easier to come legally than illegally

Q: For years you supported a path to citizenship for illegal immigrants. Now, according to your book, you no longer support that, but support a path to legal residency. Why have you changed?

BUSH: I haven't changed. The book was written to try to create a blueprint for conservatives that were reluctant to embrace comprehensive reform, to give them, perhaps, a set of views that they could embrace. I support a path to legalization or citizenship so long as the path for people that have been waiting patiently is easier and costs less, the legal entrance to our country, than illegal entrance. The worst thing that we could do is to pass a set of laws and have the exact same problem we had in the late 1980s, where there was not the enforcement and it was easier to come legally than illegally.

Source: CBS Face the Nation interview, March 10, 2013

Book Reviews

OnTheIssues excerpts political books and debates as the primary source of the materials in this book. Following are several book reviews, plus links online to additional books and debates cited in this book. These book reviews (and the books themselves) tell a lot about the priorities of the candidates (for memoirs) and about the image of the candidates (both positive and negative, for biographies written by others).

Since Jeb Bush and Rand Paul are both in the position of having had immediate relatives run for president, we include several biographies of those immediate relatives. In the context of those related biographies, we compare Rand Paul's issue stances to those of his father, Rep. Ron Paul, who ran for president in 1988, 2008, and 2012. And we compare Jeb's issue stances to those of his father, George H. W. Bush, who ran for president in 1980, 1988, and 1992; as well as those of his brother George W. Bush, who ran for president in 2000 and 2004.

Book reviews:

Additional book / debate excerpts online:

- *The Party's Over*, by Gov. Charlie Crist (R-FL), (2014)
  Includes excerpts from Jeb Bush as Florida Governor.
  www.ontheissues.org/Party_Over.htm

- *Speeches to Conservative Political Action Conference* (2013)
  Includes speeches by both Rand Paul and Jeb Bush,
  plus links to several other CPAC conferences where both spoke.
  www.ontheissues.org/2013_CPAC.htm

- *The Values Voters Summit* by the Family Research Council (2012)
  Includes excerpts from Rand Paul in the Religious Right context.
  www.ontheissues.org/2012_Values_Voters.htm

- *The Rise of Marco Rubio,* by Manuel Rogi-Franzia, (2012)
  Includes excerpts from Jeb Bush as Florida Governor.
  www.ontheissues.org/Rise_of_Rubio.htm

- Republican National Convention speeches (2012)
  Includes speeches by both Rand Paul and Jeb Bush,
  plus links to several other RNC conventions where both spoke.
  www.ontheissues.org/2012_RNC.htm

- Florida State of the State speech (2004)
  Includes speech by Jeb as Governor, plus links to other years.
  www.ontheissues.org/2004_State.htm

Book Review:
A Clear Vision to Revitalize America,
by Rand Paul (Oct. 1, 2013)

This document is a proposed budget by Senator Rand Paul. It outlines his spending priorities and hence his policy priorities.

Budgets often represent the best means of assessing political priorities: it forces "putting your money where your mouth is," i.e., actual decisions instead of just rhetoric. A budget requires deciding which programs should be cut to pay for the programs that the budget author prefers.

Rand Paul's budget is not simply a table of numbers: it outlines his political beliefs and how he came to believe them too. Washington politicians can always find evidence to support their political beliefs, since they have large research teams available. Hence *WHICH* evidence a budget cites is an excellent indicator of *WHY* the author believes what he does. Rand Paul's priorities, as expressed in this budget, include:

- p. 17-8 on trade policy:
  Accompany free trade laws with other export inducers
- p. 21-2 on educational testing:
  Washington-based metrics stifle new ideas & innovation
- p. 23-4 on education funding:
  Why tax federally to send money back to local schools?
- p. 29-30 on welfare policy:
  Poverty line is $11,490, but welfare adds $25,000
- p. 30-1 on welfare funding:
  Block grant welfare to states and communities
- p. 37 on foreign policy:
  No isolationism; but don't go abroad seeking enemies
- p. 42 on security abroad:
  Prioritize embassy security to avoid another Benghazi

Book review written March 2015
full excerpts available online at:
www.ontheissues.org/Revitalize_America.htm

Book Review: Immigration Wars:
Forging an American Solution
by Jeb Bush and Clint Bolick (March 5, 2013)

Immigration Wars is Jeb Bush's opening salvo in the battle for the 2016 presidential nomination. It addresses what Jeb sees as a key issue for the 2016 race, and a key issue for the Republican Party. If the Republicans get immigration right, they stand to gain a substantial electoral benefit; this book attempts to position Jeb to be the primary beneficiary of that electoral benefit.

"Getting immigration right" means accomplishing the following (all of which Jeb addresses):

- Addressing the 12 million illegal immigrants presently in the US so that the number gets reduced over time;

- Addressing the needs of businesses for cheap labor, which is the driving force for illegal immigration;

- Addressing those issues in a manner which is affordable under the current tight budget; and

- Doing all of the above in a manner that Hispanics consider fair and acceptable.

That last one is where the electoral benefit comes from. The illegal immigration issue, although it affects immigrants from all countries, is most important to the Hispanic community. That community compromises 16.7% of the current US population, and in 2012 voted 71% for Obama for president.

The electoral benefit comes from shifting enough of those Hispanic votes to win states which would otherwise vote for the Democratic nominee in 2016. The five states most likely to swing on the immigration issue are NM, AZ, NV, FL, and CO. Mitt Romney won only Arizona out of those five swing states in 2012. Romney winning those other four swing states in 2012, totaling 49 electoral votes, would have closed the electoral gap substantially (Romney would have won the presidency with a shift of 64 electoral votes). For the GOP nominee to win those four swing states in 2016...:

State	Electoral Votes	Percent Hispanic Population	2012 votes for Obama	2012 votes for Romney	Hispanics needed for 2016
New Mexico	5	46.3%	415,000 (53%)	336,000 (43%)	79,000 (61%)
Nevada	6	26.5%	531,000 (52%)	464,000 (46%)	68,000 (65%)
Florida	29	22.5%	4,238,000 (50%)	4,163,000 (49%)	74,300 (35%)
Colorado	9	20.7%	1,323,000 (52%)	1,185,000 (46%)	138,000 (66%)

To win those states requires that the 2016 nominee get 35% to 65% of the Hispanic vote instead of the 19% that Romney got. Those figures indicate why this issue is critical to the 2016 presidential election, and why Jeb has written this book.

Jeb Bush is uniquely well-positioned to benefit from a voting shift to Republican line in 2016. He is married to a Mexican woman, Columba, and their three children are who George Bush Sr. referred to as "the little brown ones." Jeb is fluent at Spanish and spent several years teaching English in Mexico (where he met his wife). The only other serious presidential contender positioned to benefit as much is Senator Marco Rubio—who has also proposed major immigration reform—this book is, in effect, Jeb's answer to Rubio's proposal.

That begs the question, "Wouldn't the Republican Party be wise to nominate Marco Rubio instead of Jeb Bush?" Well, maybe so on the immigration issue, but there are other issues as well. Let's summarize those issues into acceptability to the major factions of the Republican Party, and score some of the possible major candidates according to each faction. We'll score the recent GOP nominees for comparison, too:

	Mainstream GOP	Tea Party	Christian Right	Neocons	Liber-tarians
Jeb Bush	A+	B-	B	A-	B-
Marco Rubio	B	A	B	C	B-
Chris Christie	A-	B-	C	C	B-
Nikki Haley	B	A+	A	B	B-
Rand Paul	C-	A	C	D	A+
Mitt Romney	A	C	C	B-	C
Paul Ryan	B	A	B	B	C
John McCain	A	C	C	A	C
Sarah Palin	C	A	A+	A	C
G.W. Bush	A	B	A	A+	D

Jeb is acceptable to all factions of the Republican Party; no other major 2016 candidate is. Rubio is unacceptable to the neoconservatives (the faction led by Dick Cheney and Karl Rove, who mostly like Jeb because he is George's brother; Jeb's actual foreign policy stances are largely unknown). Some pundits predict that the neocons will become irrelevant by 2016, but it is more likely that they will be a major source of fundraising, as they have been in past elections, and that Jeb will win the "money primary" accordingly. Unlike the other 2016 contenders, Jeb can unite the Republican Party; all of the others will force the GOP to choose one faction over another. Gov. Nikki Haley (R, SC) also is acceptable to all factions, and we include her for that reason; but she has not yet achieved national name recognition like the others in the list.

Reaction to this book was mixed, at least from the perspective of the pundits. Many pundits pointed out that Jeb formerly stated that a pathway to citizenship was important; in this book he says it would encourage more illegal immigration, and prefers a pathway to legal residency status instead. In his book tour following this book's publication, Jeb stated that a pathway to citizenship should be available but with conditions; and that the book outlines a proposal without citizenship as a model for conservative legislation. The pundits called that sequence a double flip-flop.

But voters don't think like pundits—all they care about is that Jeb has a clear position. In particular, Hispanic voters care that the candidate advocates for a pathway to legalization, even with conditions, and even if full citizenship is disallowed—which is what Jeb has outlined. What the pundits call "flip-flopping," the voting public will likely view as "a full understanding of a complex issue."

To summarize what Jeb proposes in this book (which he does in chapter 1, entitled "A Proposal for Immigration Reform," and then details the policy and politics of that proposal for the rest of the book):

1. *Fundamental Reform*: Comprehensive interrelated approach because system as a whole is broken, and to achieve bipartisan consensus.

2. *A Demand-Driven Immigration System*: Replace overriding preference for family reunification with work-based immigration.

3. *An Increased Role for the States*: Share federal authority over immigration policy [such as] social services and providing benefits.

4. *Dealing With Current Illegal Immigrants*: We propose a path to permanent legal resident status for those who plead guilty to having entered our country illegally as adults and who have committed no additional crimes of significance.

5. *Border Security*: Broader immigration reform is an essential component of border security; we can't do one without the other.

6. *Toward a More Vibrant Future*: Getting immigration policy right will allow us to reclaim the prosperity that in recent years has eluded our grasp.

In summary, this book is an important early contribution to the 2016 race, and declares, loud and clear, that Jeb is preparing to run.

Book review written March 2013; full excerpts available online at: www.ontheissues.org/Immigration_Wars.htm

Book Review:
Government Bullies:
How Everyday Americans Are Being Harassed, Abused, and Imprisoned by the Feds, by Sen. Rand Paul (Sept. 12, 2012)

This book is tedious to read. It comprises case after case (after case after case) about wetlands, and about how the federal government took inappropriate action against the owners of those wetlands. The reader concludes that there just MUST be another side to these stories! As a result, the book feels imbalanced—like propaganda, rather than like an effective political argument. A few cases, focused on a few key issues, would have been better—and even better yet would have been interviewing the enforcing agencies to get their side of the story.

The over-focus on environmental issues contributes to the feel of imbalance. There are other sections of the book, but the first 100 pages are dedicated entirely to the EPA—that's "Part 1." Then "Part 2" brings up another 52 pages on environmental enforcement by NMFS—which is a federal agency unrelated to the EPA, but readers will not make that distinction (it's the National Marine Fisheries Service, a branch of the Department of Commerce, under separate jurisdiction than the EPA, but it's still all just environmental law, to the casual reader).

Finally, beginning on page 155, we get some issues related to the TSA, the DHS, the FDA, and the USDA. Finally, after 155 pages, this book gets interesting—because it makes some generalizations about federal activity and federal wrongdoing. Prior to mentioning those other agencies, it was unclear if Paul's argument was anti-environmentalist, anti-EPA, or just anti-Lacey Act (and other environmental laws). If the book had started with non-environmental agencies, and then applied the lessons to the EPA and NMFS, it would be more effective—and would retain more readers too!

Senator Paul is running for president in 2016, the pundits say. This book is a good start, because it outlines numerous issue stances that Paul will fight for in the Senate and will bring to the fore in 2016. The senior Paul wrote numerous heavy-duty policy books; this is the first pure policy book by the junior Paul (he wrote a book on the Tea Party, but its focus was politics, not policy). We hope that Senator Paul will write more (and better!) books prior to 2016. The Paulistas who adored Senator Paul's father will enjoy this book—but it's just too hard to read for the typical reader.

Book review written Oct. 2013;
            full excerpts available online at:
                www.ontheissues.org/Government_Bullies.htm

Book Review: Now Or Never:
Saving America from Economic Collapse
by Sen. Jim DeMint, R-SC (Jan. 10, 2012)

Sen. DeMint is the leader of the Senate Tea Party; he is referred to by some pundits as "Senator Tea Party" and helped the other Tea Party-oriented Senators get elected. This book describes the growth of the Tea Party in the U.S. Senate. (DeMint also describes himself as "Senator No," p. 213, because he votes "No" so often, but that's not as relevant a moniker for this book!)

Sen. Rand Paul, one of the Senators assisted in his election by DeMint, writes in the Foreword to the book (several other Tea Party Senators write other sections): "During the debt ceiling debate, the media began to wonder if the Tea Party was now in control of Washington. If only this were true. In the following pages, Sen. DeMint points the way forward." (p. xv)

Sen. DeMint describes the book's purpose as more citizen-oriented: "This book will equip you with everything you need to know to help save our country. Please read it and share it with others, and joint he fight for freedom." (p. xxix)

The name of the book, "Now Or Never," refers to two passages in the book, one communication-based and one partisan-based. On successful communication, DeMint writes, "Voters have to believe we are telling the truth when we say, 'It's now or never to save America.' Our message must be clear and persuasive." (p. 188, but that message is a hard-sell because it's repeated in just about every election). On the partisan side, DeMint writes, "Despite the devastating impact of Obama's policies, nearly half of Americans still support his reelection. Those who know better must be ready to fight for freedom in 2012—because it really is now or never." (p. 192, but that message has the same problem as the first one, that every presidential opponent describes every election that way.

The underlying purpose of this book, as we see it, is to popularize the Senate Conservatives Fund (pp. 215ff), the PAC founded by Sen. DeMint to fund conservative Senate candidates. DeMint is well-known for funding Tea Party-oriented GOP primary candidates who take on establishment Republicans. Two are cited heavily in this book. Tea Party favorite Rand Paul won the 2010 Kentucky GOP primary against the Republican establishment candidate Trey Grayson; Sen. Paul wrote the Foreword to this book. And Tea Party hero Pat Toomey won the 2010 Pennsylvania GOP primary by scaring away the RINO Arlen Specter; Sen. Toomey wrote the introduction to Chapter One.

This book joins our growing collection of Tea Party literature. It's tough to find a generally-accepted definition of the Tea Party's beliefs. This book establishes those beliefs in members of the Senate who also claim membership in the Tea Party. See our book list below for the rest of our Tea Party collection.

Book review written June 2012;
full excerpts available online at:
www.ontheissues.org/Now_or_Never.htm

Book Review:
The Tea Party Goes to Washington,
by Rand Paul (Feb. 22, 2011)

Sen. Paul claims (pp. 86-88) that he was the first Tea Party candidate to win a statewide race. Well, that's an exciting statement, but only true if one looks at it in just the right way. Mike Lee was elected statewide in Utah on the same night, but one time zone west of Paul's Kentucky, so technically Paul was first. Marco Rubio was also elected statewide in Florida on the same night, and in the same pair of time zones, but the polls in Florida closed later than those in Kentucky, so again Paul is technically correct. Scott Brown was elected statewide in Massachusetts months earlier, in an important Tea Party victory, but Sen. Brown does not claim the Tea Party mantle for himself. Nevertheless, Sen. Paul is an important national voice of the Tea Party movement.

So what does Rand Paul believe as Tea Party spokesperson? And more importantly, what does the Tea Party "believe," if one can attribute issue stances to a grassroots organization? Paul hated George W. Bush (p. 52), characterizing his presidency as spendthrift and warmongering; clearly most Tea Party members agree with that. Paul still hated Bush when McCain ran for president in 2008 (p. 82), and his anti-Bush feelings rubbed off onto McCain electorally. That implies that the only reason McCain didn't fare even worse in the 2008 election is that he picked the Tea Party darling Sarah Palin as his running mate, and got *SOME* Tea Party votes as a result. Mostly Paul hates the neoconservatives (p. 150) who dominated Bush's cabinet, and says the Tea Party hates the neocons too.

Hence Sen. Paul positions the Tea Party as part of the split in the Republican Party between the neocons and the libertarians, claiming the Tea Party is on the libertarian side. The key distinction in that split is whether one believes in a massive defense buildup: the neocons do; the libertarians don't. That distinction does not necessarily apply to the majority of the Tea Party, however: Sarah Palin (who endorsed Sen. Paul, p. 78) would build up the military; so would Sens. Lee, Brown, and Rubio, three Tea Party Senators. The key vote that would occur is whether to accept military cuts as part of a big budget cut package: Paul would certainly vote yes; those other senators *MIGHT* vote yes, unlike neocon Senators (like McCain) who would certainly vote no.

So is Sen. Paul wrong? Well, we consider his opinion more like "guidance" for where he'd *LIKE* the Tea Party to go. Of course some Tea Partiers do support military cuts, especially as part of a budget cut package. But we do think Paul has transferred his own view onto the Tea Party. Why would he do that? Let me illustrate with an interview I conducted with David Walker, the former Comptroller General of the United States. The purpose of the interview was to ascertain Walker's issue stances for our VoteMatch quiz; after an hour-long verbal interview, I wrote up my interpretation of his answers to our 20-question quiz. Upon Walker's review, we determined that I had interpreted 3 out of 20 incorrectly—and in all three cases, I transferred my own viewpoint onto Mr. Walker. It's not that I'm a bad interviewer—that's human nature—we interpret what we want to hear. I think Sen. Paul has done the same with the Tea Party's stance on military cuts—Sen. Paul believes in military cuts, and assumes that the Tea Party believes the same. But my editing process corrected my personal misinterpretations of David Walker's positions—there is no editing process for the Tea Party movement, so we'll have to wait and see if others agree with Sen. Paul or not.

That begs the question about whether Sen. Paul is a libertarian or not. He notes (p. 78) that his *OPPONENTS* call him a libertarian, but that he's pro-life, anti-gay-marriage, and several other stances that are counter to libertarian ideals. He is the son of Rep. Ron Paul, the libertarian standard-bearer for many years now, so many people assume that Rand Paul is just as libertarian as his father. One can see an overview by observing our VoteMatch table for the two of them side-by-side, along with the VoteMatch table for the Libertarian Party and the Tea Party (graphics next page). In summary:

- Rand Paul is less libertarian than Ron Paul

- Rand Paul is a lot less libertarian than the Libertarian Party (and so is Ron Paul; in other words, neither are pure libertarians)

- Rand Paul is much more libertarian than the Tea Party.

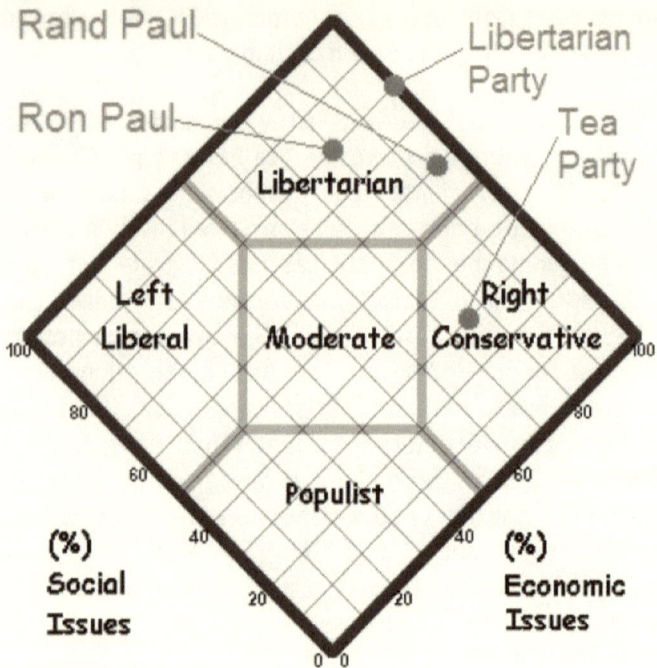

Rand Paul

Ron Paul

Libertarian Party

Tea Party

Libertarian

Left Liberal

Moderate

Right Conservative

100   100

80   80

60   60

Populist

(%)
Social
Issues

40   40

20   20

(%)
Economic
Issues

0 0

VoteMatch political philosophy ratings:
- Rand Paul is a Conservative-Leaning Libertarian
- Rand Paul is a Moderate Libertarian
- The Libertarian Party is Hard-Core Libertarian
- The Tea Party is Libertarian-Leaning Moderate Conservative

Both the senior and junior Paul count as libertarian by our VoteMatch labeling; certainly Ron Paul is *MORE* libertarian, but Rand Paul can claim that also. We include in the VoteMatch analysis our still-growing Tea Party summary: the Tea Party is decidedly *NOT* libertarian. Rand Paul is placed on our two-dimensional political spectrum just about halfway between the Tea Party and the Libertarian Party—meaning that he can make a legitimate claim to representing both constituencies.

Book review written July 2012;
VoteMatch tables updated February 2015;
full excerpts available online at:
www.ontheissues.org/Tea_Party_Goes.htm

Book Review: End the Fed:
by Rep. Ron Paul (Sept. 29, 2010)

Economics is known as "the dismal science." Rep. Ron Paul does his best in this book to explain economics entertainingly, but it's a pretty dismal book. Paul does a fine job explaining economics as well as his policy prescriptions for the economic future—but the "dismal science" topic disallows Paul's usual entertaining style. If you want to understand this economic crisis, plow through this book. But if you want an entertaining book, try Paul's other books.

The title "End the Fed" derives from a chanting crowd during the 2008 election: "The title of this book comes from a slogan that can be heard at rallies all around the country. I first heard it at the University of Michigan in October 2007. When I mentioned monetary policy, a small group chanted, 'End the Fed! End the Fed!' The whole crowd of 4,000 took up the call. Many held up burning dollar bills, as if to say to the central bank, you have done enough damage: your time is up." (p. 4)

Back to the dismal science: Some of Paul's points:

- The Fed creates money out of thin air, as opposed to basing it on gold. (pp. 2-3)

- The Fed's money monopoly depreciates the dollar (pp. 6-7)

- The Fed was founded in 1924 to end all business cycles & panics, but obviously has not (pp. 24-27)

- We should restore the gold standard (backing dollars with gold) which Nixon ended in 1971 (pp. 44-46)

Paul goes into much more technical detail on many other issues too—he really does explain how money works; how the Fed manipulates the system; and why politicians prefer to keep the system that way. If you're going to study the dismal science, and don't mind the libertarian take, this book really is the best way to learn it!

Book review written June 2011;
full excerpts available online at:
www.ontheissues.org/End_Fed.htm

Updated Book Review for 2016 race:

The key question for the 2016 Republican primaries is whether the Paulistas will accept Rand Paul as a replacement for Ron Paul. Without that support, Rand Paul cannot hope to win the primary, since that group of fervent supporters created both Ron Paul's volunteer staff and his grassroots power.

To illustrate the fervency of that grassroots power, online surveys in 2012 routinely had to report their results in two batches: one with Ron Paul, who would almost always win any online survey because the Paulistas would find it and flood it with their votes; and then one report without Ron Paul, trying to gauge the rest of the field outside of the Paulistas. That represented real power: Ron Paul was certain to be mentioned in any news article about any online survey.

Rand Paul will need that same army. Without the Paulista army, Rand Paul would have to rely on Tea Party support. While he is popular among the Tea Party, there are other Tea Party candidates running as well: the likely field includes Tea Party favorites such as Dr. Ben Carson, Gov. Scott Walker, Sen. Ted Cruz, and Sen. Marco Rubio. Even if Rand Paul were equal in popularity with those other candidates, he would still be splitting the Tea Party vote five ways. Rand Paul can count on Tea Party support in the general election, but not in the primary election. For the GOP primary, Rand Paul needs the Paulistas.

Many of Ron Paul's supporters were unique in supporting *ONLY* Ron Paul—there was no splitting of the vote. His supporters came in two groups: those based on economic issues (the "End the Fed" crowd) and those based on opposing military intervention (the "End the War" crowd). Ron Paul's book explores the economic issues—and we compare those to Rand Paul's views below—so we'll explore a bit further in this book review about the military issues.

For full disclosure, I voted for Ron Paul in the 2012 GOP primary, based on his anti-war stance. I don't call myself a Paulista, but I voted in my share of online surveys in favor of Ron Paul, and attended a couple of local rallies. I am a registered Independent, and call myself a progressive, and Ron Paul got my vote in 2012 because he was unambiguously the most anti-war of any candidate in any party. I felt my vote sent a message—get the U.S. out of both Iraq and Afghanistan—to both the rest of the GOP field and to President Obama. On the philosophy of "End the Fed," I appreciated Ron Paul's bringing an important unheard issue to the electorate, but I don't actually want to end the Fed. I think my viewpoint is representative of the "End the War" crowd of Ron Paul supporters.

Rand Paul will likely accomplish that same set of criteria: he will capture the "End the Fed" crowd, as well as the "End the War" crowd. Rand Paul is by far the most anti-war of anyone in the Republican primary field, and more anti-war than Hillary Clinton as well (in 2016, "anti-war" means "stay out of Iran, Syria, Ukraine, and North Korea"—the places change, but the policy remains the same). There will likely be an anti-war progressive running in the Democratic primary—most likely Sen. Bernie Sanders although many people talk about Sen. Elizabeth Warren—and hence the "End the War" crowd will have to choose in which primary to vote. But for those choosing Republican on anti-war grounds, Rand Paul is the clear choice. For those who want to "End the Fed…"

Where Rand Paul and Ron Paul agree on Economic issues

- Both agree on restricting the Federal Reserve
- Both support Balanced Budget Amendment
- Both oppose Corporate welfare
- Both oppose income tax

Where Rand Paul and Ron Paul disagree on Economic issues

	Ron Paul	Rand Paul
Federal Reserve	End the Fed	Audit the Fed
Free Trade:	Hard core support	Support with incentives
Social Security:	End Social Security	Fix Social Security
Welfare & Poverty:	It's unconstitutional	It perpetuates poverty

Book Review: Jeb Bush:
Aggressive Conservatism in Florida
by Robert E. Crew, Jr. (Dec. 11, 2009)

This book is an academic analysis of Jeb Bush's political philosophy and policy actions during his two gubernatorial terms. The emphasis is on "academic": the author is a professor of political science at Florida State University. Hence this book does not read like a typical political book at all—it reads like a classroom study, with well-documented references and extensive footnotes.

Like any academic treatise, the professor injects lots of history and political theory:

- The history of Florida politics (converting from Democrat to Republican as part of the GOP "Southern Strategy" since the 1960s, pp. xiii-xvii);

- The history of the Florida legislature (8-year term limits passed in 1992, and hence took full effect in 2000, one year after during Jeb's first inauguration in 1999; that greatly empowered the Executive branch relative to the Legislative branch, pp. 64-65).

- A theory of privatization as a core principle of government (pp. 116-7 as a philosophy; p. 30 as a policy goal of reducing state worker headcounts).

- The theory of "aggressive conservatism," as indicated in the book's subtitle, permeates the book, even though Jeb himself never uttered the phrase (it presumably counters George W. Bush's phrase "compassionate conservatism"). An example of the heavily academic verbiage on this topic: "The theory of conserv-atism adopted by Jeb Bush was relentlessly consistent and carried with it an almost canonical list of specific agenda items to be checked off, many of which were viewed as moral absolutes rather than options open to debate and alteration." (p. 24)

The massive overuse of the passive voice, so common in academia, often leaves the reader struggling to figure out who exactly is doing what. That sentence from p. 24 could be translated as, "Bush did all the usual things that conservatives do, and did them because he thought they were the right thing to do, and wouldn't take 'no' for an answer." Massive parsing is required, when the passive voice is so massively overused. Here's the worst example (which we promise to parse and illustrate, so don't panic like we did):

> A variety of empirical measures permit an objective assessment of the political legacy left by a governor. These include the extent to which a political figure affects partisan attachments among citizens, and the degree to which he or she improves the electoral fortunes of his or her party.... An examination of these measures in Florida reinforces the view that Governor Bush left a modest political legacy in the state.

We *THINK* that means, "Political scientists measure governors by how well their party does, and by how well others of their party do, too; Bush didn't do so well by either measurement." In other words, fewer Floridians registered as Republicans after Jeb than did before Jeb, and the Republican Party of Florida's elective position got weaker as well. But the author substantiates that Jeb did accomplish his philosophical goals, using a massively academic chart:

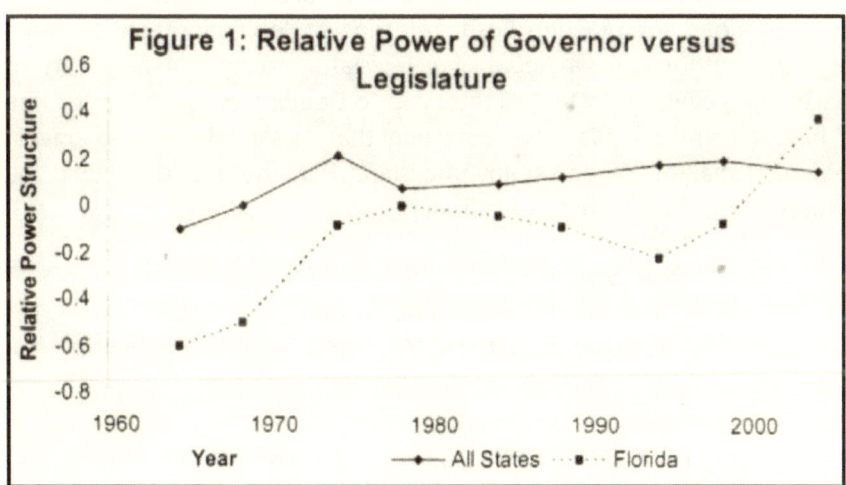

That chart (p. 68) indicates that when Jeb took office in 1999, the Florida governorship became a stronger office than the national average, whereas before Jeb the Florida legislature was the stronger branch. But if one reads the several paragraphs accompanying the chart, the author clarifies that the chart summarizes a multi-year survey of Florida executive branch officials. In other words, this chart indicates what state workers *THINK* about legislative power in Florida compared to other states—not anything that Jeb actually did, measured in some objective manner, or even anything that Jeb said.

Reading the rest of the book, astute readers might note that the big swing in power came about because of the implementation of legislative term limits, which was passed in 1992 (the turning point of the chart) and threw out many long-time legislators in 2000 (pp. 64-65). The author doesn't make that connection—leaving it to the astuteness of the reader, or more likely leaving the reader to incorrectly assume that Jeb *CAUSED* the change.

I guess that's what "political science" means: making charts that readers must really study to understand. For most readers, that's way too academic—it'd be better to explain the political implications directly, rather than leaving so much to inference. We don't think the author is biased against Jeb—just too biased towards academia. But the author assuredly does not *LIKE* Jeb Bush: referring to Jeb's nickname as "King Jeb," the author cites a Republican legislator saying, "In his heart of hearts, the governor prefers dictatorship to Democracy" (p. 171). It's fine to have an anti-Jeb bias—we conclude that this book is a reasonably unbiased analysis of Jeb's governorship. But the reader should be prepared for an adventure in academia!

Book review written Dec. 2012;
full excerpts available online at:
www.ontheissues.org/Aggressive_Conservatism.htm

Book Review: Jeb: America's Next Bush:
His Florida Years and
What They Mean For the Nation,
by S.V. Dáte (February 15, 2007)

The author of "America's Next Bush," Shirish V. Dáte, is a Tallahassee journalist who covers Florida state government for the Associated Press and the Palm Beach Post. He does not like Jeb Bush, and he opens his preface with the warning, "Jeb Bush is going to hate this book." Hence this book is a critic's perspective on Bush's governorship, and of Bush's world view in general. Dáte does his share of bashing George W. Bush and George Bush Sr., too, (he claims the Bush family is "bent on global domination," p. xvi), in the context of analyzing why Jeb was "Born To Rule" as the "King Of Florida" (those are two chapter titles!).

However, Dáte is careful to balance his critiques with credit where credit is due. He praises Jeb (and points out the rest of Florida's praise) for Jeb's handling of disastrous hurricanes in 2005 (pp. 21-22 and again about Hurricane Katrina on pp. 168-169). He credits Jeb with registering 88,000 Hispanic voters in the 1980s, as part of his father's presidential campaign (Hispanics vote overwhelmingly Democratic, except in Florida, where Cubans overwhelmingly vote Republican). And he acknowledges that Jeb's use of $310 million in budget stimulus funds in 2003 were used well (for a biotech center) even though Dáte and others disagreed at the time. Dáte's balance, by praising some items and criticizing others, does make his criticisms seem more valid.

And Dáte's criticisms are very critical indeed. He feels that Jeb considers himself "Prince Jeb," (the title of Chapter 1) entitled to rule without dissent from the legislature or the judicial branch (and without much dissent possible from the public, since Jeb opposed the "Sunshine Laws," p. 41-42). Worse, Dáte accuses Jeb of receiving a large fortune from the 1980s Savings & Loan bailout (the same one which banned his brother Neil Bush from politics)—that Jeb benefited to the tune of $4 million from an S&L bailout, despite Jeb's protests of no wrongdoing. And Dáte gleefully details every time Jeb apologized over the years, such as when he overdid his criticism of his opponent for weakness on the death penalty in a TV ad (pp. 112-113).

The problem with Dáte's criticism is when he offers his own opinions, which is ok, but in criticizing those who oppose his own opinion, he isn't clear when the opponent is Jeb and when it is not. For example, Dáte describes his own stance against Jeb's proposed healthcare privatization (pp. 163-164) by defending whether Medicare and Medicaid are socialistic—but Jeb never described Medicare and Medicaid as "socialistic." Similarly, Dáte criticizes those who fly the Confederate flag, on grounds of "Southern heritage," as racist—for a page and a half (pp. 193-194)—before letting the reader know that Jeb *took down* the Confederate flag from the Florida Capitol (p. 195)—and did it quietly, to avoid a hullabaloo over "Southern heritage."

Overall, Dáte is reasonably journalistic in his criticism (usually), i.e. readers can read this book as valid criticism, not as simple Bush-bashing. But the reader needs to read carefully to avoid mixing up Dáte's opinions with those of Jeb or Jeb's opponents. Especially as one approaches the end of the book, where later chapters are less reporting and more speculation (about a possible presidential run). If Jeb runs for president in 2016, this will be an important book for his opponents to read, as background for how Jeb operated in Florida and as a prediction for how he will behave as a presidential candidate and as president. But before 2016, we hope there will be better books about Jeb that don't require the reader to be quite as cautious.

Book review written Dec. 2012; full excerpts available online at:
www.ontheissues.org/Next_Bush.htm

Book Review: My Father, My President:
A Personal Account
of the Life of George H. W. Bush
by Doro Bush Koch (Oct. 6, 2006)

Doro Bush Koch, the author of this memoir, is the younger sister of Governor Jeb Bush & President George W. Bush, and the daughter of President George H. W. Bush Sr. The book focuses on her father, but includes substantial personal insight into her two brothers as well. She has no political ambitions of her own, so this memoir represents the official Bush family line, without the bias inherent in autobiography. Therefore this book makes an interesting contrast to *All the Best*, President George H. W. Bush Sr.'s memoir, and *Decision Points*, President George W. Bush Jr.'s memoir.

Doro has her own unique insight into the three protagonists, and adds to her personal perspective that of numerous high-ranking aides, whom she cites extensively. Unlike with Kitty Kelley's joint biography of the same three protagonists, the high-ranking aides knew they could trust Doro to portray the Bushes in a sympathetic light (which Kitty Kelley often did not do), and hence were more forthcoming.

While there is some value to reading a presidential memoir by a "sympathetic insider," the book does have a larger purpose. Besides describing the official Bush family line on key historical events, this book also establishes the official Bush family legacy—i.e., how the Bushes want us to view Bush 41's and Bush 43's presidencies. And perhaps even more importantly, this book establishes the official Bush family dynasty—how the Bushes want us to perceive their future candidates (specifically, Jeb Bush for President, and George P. Bush for some other office later).

There is not a lot of material about Jeb, however—the book, as promised in its title and subtitle, focuses on Doro's father. For Jeb's future campaigns, this book sets more of a tone than a policy agenda. That tone could be summarized as the "Bush Political Doctrine:" maintain bipartisanship; exercise restrained prudence in important decisions;

remain resolute and loyal. All three of the protagonists want voters and historians to believe that they all followed all of those criteria whenever possible. Whether those are actually true of any of the three politicians in any given situation is up to the reader to decide—Doro makes the case here for just one side.

Book review written Jan. 2013;
full excerpts available online at:
www.ontheissues.org/Father_President.htm

Book Review: The Family:
The Real Story of the Bush Dynasty
by Kitty Kelley (Sept. 14, 2004)

This is a joint biography of President George H. W. Bush Sr., and his son President George W. Bush Jr. It's also a briefer biography of Governor Jeb Bush (George W.'s brother) and Senator Prescott Bush (George H.'s father).

Of primary importance in understanding this biography is the author—Kitty Kelley, who was also the biographer for Jackie Onassis, Nancy Reagan, Frank Sinatra, and her other famous joint biography of the British royal family. In particular, Nancy Reagan told the Bush family to *NOT* participate with Kitty Kelley, because Kelley had some negative things to say about Nancy Reagan. Kelley has many, many negative things to say about the Bush family —perhaps more so because they listened to Nancy Reagan and forced Kelley to write an unauthorized biography.

Kelley digs up a lot of dirt about the senior President Bush in this book. (She digs up a lot of dirt about the junior President Bush too, but most of that dirt was already well-known.) For the senior President Bush,

Kelley digs back to the 1960s, when Bush Sr. ran for Congress and the Senate in Texas.

At issue was that Bush was a "progressive Republican" in the mold of other Republican New Englanders like Sen. Olympia Snowe (R, ME) and Gov. Linc Chafee (R, RI). When Bush moved from New England to Texas, he had to change some of his stances in order to be eligible for high office—in particular on civil rights, contraception, and other social issues. Then when he ran as Reagan's Vice President in 1990, he had to change his stances again, to fit better with Reagan.

Kelley undertakes the clean method of digging up Bush's issue stances from old elections and comparing them to his current stances— that's real reporting, not gossip and not attacking. Readers might know Kitty Kelley from her past at *People* magazine and other gossip-focused reporting—and hence might (incorrectly) assume that this is a gossip-oriented biography. Kelley does summarize the gossip of the day—about Bush Senior's "girlfriend" while in office (never fully substantiated) and Bush Junior's well-known peccadilloes as well. But the real reporting vastly overwhelms the gossip—Kelley establishes herself as a serious biographer and a serious political reporter.

Book review written April 2012;
full excerpts available online at:
www.ontheissues.org/Kitty_Kelley.htm

Book Review:
The Faith of George W. Bush,
by Stephen Mansfield (April 30, 2004)

This book is about George W. Bush's faith as a candidate and president, but also about the faith of George H. W. Bush, the father. The two are intertwined, of course, since Bush Sr. chose Bush Jr.'s early church experiences. But the book outlines how their presidential politics continued that intertwining in adulthood.

The author claims (p. xiv) to have written this book because "the matter of his religious faith... is another likely pillar of George W. Bush's legacy." While that is not true for Bush Sr., the author does spend a lot of ink on the earlier president too. The author details (p. 19) how Bush Sr. considered his faith to be "personal," while Bush Jr., as indicated by the quote above, considered his faith to be a critical component of his policymaking.

This book is the first of a series by Stephen Mansfield on the faith of presidents and presidential candidates. Mansfield later authored The Faith of Barack Obama (2008) and The Faith and Values of Sarah Palin (2010). Mansfield also writes faith-oriented biographies about non-politicians; but we hope he continues this insightful series on many more candidates.

Book review written Oct. 2011;
full excerpts available online at:
www.ontheissues.org/Hard_Choices.htm

Updated Book Review for 2016 race:

At issue in the upcoming 2016 election is what would be in a book entitled, *The Faith of Jeb Bush*. Assuming that issue arises—and it most certainly will, after the electorate spent so much of 2012 exploring the Mormonism of Mitt Romney and the habits of Barack Obama's pastor (Rev. Jeremiah Wright, remember?)—we expect the same in 2016. We outline below the policy differences between Jeb, his brother, and his father.

Jeb has one important distinction from the past two Presidents Bush: they were members of the Episcopalian Church, while Jeb is a Catholic. Jeb converted in 1995 to his wife Columba's religion. If elected, Jeb would be only the second Catholic President, after John F. Kennedy. Catholicism played an important role in Kennedy's 1960 election; but questions about Jeb's status as the would-be second Catholic president will likely take a back seat to issues about Hillary's status as the would-be first female president, and about Rand Paul's status as the would-be first libertarian president in more than a century.

Where George W. Bush, Jeb Bush, & George Bush Sr. agree on Social issues

- All are hard-core pro-life
- All support faith-based social services
- All support character education
- All support abstinence education
- All support family values
- All support school vouchers

Where George W. Bush, Jeb Bush, & George Bush Sr. disagree on Social issues

	George W. Bush	Jeb Bush	George Bush Sr.
Stem Cells:	Compromised on stem cells	Hard core against stem cells	(No stance on stem cells)
Gay rights:	Hard-core for traditional marriage	Moderate for traditional marriage	Moderate for gay rights
Welfare:	Replace welfare with self-help	Replace welfare with work	Replace welfare with enterprise zones
Conservation:	Private land stewardship	State-run conservation	Personal conservation

Book Review: Fortunate Son
George W. Bush and the Making of an American President, by J. H. Hatfield (Dec. 12, 2002)

This book is a negative biography of George W. Bush—very negative. So negative that Bush attacked the author—and hence the author became the controversy about this book, rather than the content of the book. At issue is the accusation that Bush was arrested for cocaine usage decades ago; Bush's allies responded by alleging that the author was arrested for even worse misdeeds. The counter-accusations against the author (and whether Bush was involved with them) deflected attention from the accusation against Bush—which perhaps was the purpose of the counter-accusation, if one is a cynic.

Is attacking the author a good idea? Or more relevantly, is it good politics? This book was published just prior to the 2000 election; we have two examples for comparison, in the two subsequent elections. Bush suffered electorally because of the cocaine accusation—but it never became enough of a full-fledged issue to lose him the election. In other words, the strategy of attacking the author worked.

In the 2004 election, John Kerry was similarly accused of horrendous behavior in what became known as the Swift Boat attack. Many Kerry allies attacked that book's author, Jerome Corsi, as unreliable, but Kerry himself did not respond. Kerry's lack of response is widely credited with contributing to his 2004 election loss. In other words, Kerry ignored Bush's lesson of responding by counter-attack, and paid the consequences.

After the 2008 election, Sarah Palin was the subject of an unfriendly biography called The Rogue, by Joe McGinnis. That author moved in next door to the Palins' home in Wasilla, Alaska. Palin made the author' the issue—she attacked him for invasion of privacy, and by the time the book was published, the book's content had become irrelevant— only the author's action in writing the book mattered. In other words, Palin took Bush's lesson and responded by counter-attack, and reaped the benefits.

So what about the content of this book? Why did Bush attack the author here, and not, say, the equally negative biographies *Shrub* or *Worse Than Watergate*? We think it's because this author went too far. Rather than restricting his attack to Bush's actions, the author questioned the entire Bush family. The Bushes feel entitled to high office, the author claims on pp. 2-5, because they feel like America's aristocracy.

The author goes on to attack George H. W. Bush too: questioning his actions in getting shot down over the Pacific in 1945. The author claims (pp. 306-17) that Bush Sr. ejected prematurely, and could have saved the other crew members from death. (The US Navy disagreed, and awarded Bush the Distinguished Flying Cross for that incident, as the author notes on p. 9). That sort of generic anti-Bush attack probably riled up the Bush family enough to go after the author—and it certainly feels to the reader like the author overstepped the bounds of journalistic propriety.

We excerpt this book now, in preparation for the 2016 election, because the author would certainly include Jeb Bush as subject to the negative aspects of the Bush family legacy. We can anticipate a similar attack book, and a similar counter-attack, coming soon.

> *Book review written January 2013;*
> *full excerpts available online at:*
> *www.ontheissues.org/Fortunate_Son.htm*

Updated Book Review for 2016 race:

At issue in the upcoming 2016 election is whether Jeb suffers from a similar sense of entitlement as George. In other words, is Jeb, too, a "Fortunate Son"? Presumably the author of *Fortunate Son* might include Jeb and any other members of the Bush family legacy: but let's look at some key facts about the two brothers' background of "entitlement":

- Jeb has no issues about his military service; he registered for the draft in 1971, but never got drafted because Vietnam was winding down. George Sr. served in WWII (with controversial medals, according to Hatfield) while George Jr. served stateside during Vietnam (by influence-peddling, according to Hatfield).

- Jeb was defeated for governor of Florida in 1994, then came back to win in 1998. Similarly, George Sr. was defeated in his first race for Congress in 1964, then came back to win in 1966. George Jr., on the other hand, won his first election for Governor in 1994, and never lost an election.

- Jeb graduated from the University of Texas at Austin; George Sr. graduated from Yale; and George Jr. graduated from Yale and Harvard.

Are those indicative that Jeb has less of a sense of entitlement than his father or brother? We'll let the reader decide, based on how those backgrounds translate into policy stances on entitlement-based economic and domestic issues:

Where George W. Bush, Jeb Bush, & George Bush Sr. agree on Economic / Domestic issues

- All agree on tax cuts
- All agree on federal spending cuts
- All agree on gun rights
- All agree on pursuing War on Drugs

Where George W. Bush, Jeb Bush, & George Bush Sr. disagree on Economic / Domestic issues

	George W. Bush	Jeb Bush	George Bush Sr.
Affirmative Action:	Affirmative access	Dismantle affirmative action	No quotas
Health Care:	Personal choice	Oppose ObamaCare	Optional Medicaid
Mandatory Sentencing:	Tough on crime	Alternatives to punishment	Limit appeals
Energy:	Drill offshore	Don't drill offshore	Pioneered drilling offshore

Book Review: Profiles in Character:
by Jeb Bush & Brian Yablonski

(Jan. 1996)

This book was written in 1995, after Jeb Bush had narrowly lost the 1994 Florida gubernatorial election, and before he won the 1998 election. In other words, it outlines Jeb's policy stances with the focus on addressing issues he thought contributed to his 1994 loss and would contribute to his 1998 victory. The book is published by "The Foundation for Florida's Future," which is a think tank that Jeb founded after the 1994 loss. In other words, Jeb's Foundation was founded to publish this book, in conjunction with other projects focused on winning the next time around. Of course, those methods worked, and Jeb overwhelmingly won the 1998 election (and even more overwhelmingly won his 2002 re-election).

The title of this book is a take-off on John F. Kennedy's pre-presidential book, *Profiles in Courage*. Jeb's framing mechanism, focusing on "character" instead of "courage," implies that Jeb considers character the most important attribute of leadership, where JFK considered courage the most important attribute. JFK's concept of "Profiles" as an organizing theme continues its relevance, as illustrated by Caroline Kennedy's 2003 book *Profiles in Courage For Our Time*. All of these "Profile" books focus on individual inspirational stories.

We review this book in preparation for the 2016 presidential race. While the issue stances are from a different context (a gubernatorial run) and a different era (before Jeb's brother was elected President), they are relevant for 2016 because they show the longevity of Jeb's beliefs. In other words, voters can compare Jeb's issue stances from 1995 to those he holds closer to 2016. We summarize some of the similarities and differences:

- *Abortion:* In 1995, Jeb went on record calling abortion a moral issue. As governor, Jeb focused on more practical matters such as banning stem cell research.

- *Gay Rights:* In 1995, Jeb called the gay rights movement a "modern victim movement." As governor, Jeb did not push the issue (as he has not pushed other divisive social issues).

- *Corporations:* In 1995, Jeb used the term "corporate welfare," a term usually used by anti-corporate populists. As governor, Jeb pushed two major programs that could be considered corporate welfare: using state tax money for "Touchdown Jacksonville" (a Florida NFL team) and using federal stimulus money for the Scripps biotech center. Both of those projects were widely praised, but Jeb certainly did change his view on corporate welfare.

- *Crime:* In 1995, Jeb cited the "trivialization of crime"; as governor, he focused heavily on "tough-on-crime" enforcement.

- *Education:* In 1995, Jeb focused on "grade inflation"; but as governor, he focused on charter schools and education vouchers.

- *Welfare:* In 1995, Jeb proposed making welfare "shameful"; as governor, he pushed for faith-based organizations to provide welfare services.

Those differences are more about how the issues are framed: In 1995, Jeb used "character" as an organizing theme, and framed all of the issues as aspects of morals and values. As governor, Jeb had to actually govern, and hence had to translate those thematic issues into practical policy. This book demonstrates Jeb's consistency over the years, more than providing evidence of changing stances.

We presume Jeb will write another policy book in preparation for the 2016 presidential race (if Jeb authors a book in 2013 or 2014, that is strong evidence that he is planning to run). Until then, this book is all we can go by.

Book review written Dec. 2012;
full excerpts available online at:
www.ontheissues.org/Profiles_In_Character.htm

Book Review: Freedom Under Siege:
The US Constitution After 200-Plus Years
by Rep. Ron Paul
(first published 1987; reprinted Nov. 2007)

This book was written in 1987 and re-released for Paul's presidential campaign in 2007. It has no 2007 update, unfortunately, so we have to infer that Rep. Paul still subscribes to all of his policy prescriptions from 20 years ago. The theme of this book is that big government is reducing our personal freedom, slowing our economy, and ultimately will destroy the country.

This book will be of interest to people who want a deeper understanding of what libertarians are talking about, and why Rep. Paul has generated such a large army of "Paulistas" in his presidential campaign. Rep. Paul's libertarian philosophy is well-documented here, although he would prefer the term "constitutionalist," meaning one who strictly follows the Constitution.

The book consists of four chapters:

- *Individual Rights:* This topic spans topics from morality to gun control, and we excerpt it heavily. Rep. Paul's thesis is: follow the Constitution, or follow the Amendment process if you don't like what's in the Constitution.

- *Foreign Policy:* This topic is covered in more detail in Paul's 2007 book, A Foreign Policy of Freedom. We excerpt it heavily to contrast to Rep. Paul's current statements on Iraq (anyone who knows Rep. Paul's level of consistency on this topic will know that by "compare" we mean "substantiate that he has indeed held the same views for 20 years now.")

- *The Military Draft:* This topic seems very outdated now, so we include just one representative excerpt. Rep. Paul makes only passing reference to the concept of "National Service," which would be the modern equivalent of this topic.

- **_Sound Money is Gold:_** This topic is covered in more detail in Rep. Paul's 1981 book, Gold, Peace, and Prosperity. We include a couple of excerpts and refer more interested readers to that source.

Book review written Dec. 2007;
   full excerpts available online at:
      www.ontheissues.org/Freedom_Under_Siege.htm

Updated Book Review for 2016 race:

Ron Paul re-published this book when preparing his 2008 presidential run, as the basic statement of his political philosophy; for the 2016 race, the question is whether Rand Paul ascribes to the same basic political philosophy.

In general, Rand Paul is a moderate version of Ron Paul. In other words, Rand Paul is a version of a libertarian who actually is in power and has to govern, rather than just assert a extremist or purist view of the world. For example, it's easy for Ron Paul to talk about returning to the Gold Standard, because he was never actually in a position to make it happen (he introduced bills to do so, but his purpose was to educate people about the issue, with no expectation that the bill would ever pass). Rand Paul introduces bills that he hopes will actually pass (sometimes), and hence has to actually lay out a workable plan for the bill's execution.

That distinction—philosophizing vs. governing—happens a lot in Congress, especially in 2015 where the Congress is Republican and the president is Democratic. Congress can pass numerous bills that express their philosophy, knowing that President Obama will veto the bills, so it doesn't really matter if the bill has a workable plan. Sometimes, in 2013-2014, the Republican House would pass a non-workable bill because they knew the Democratic Senate would never pass it. For example, the House passed dozens of bills overturning ObamaCare (with no plans to replace it), and the Senate rejected the bills. The new Congress may pass some similar bills—including Senate passage—knowing a veto will follow.

Knowing that your bill will fail means you are free to express your philosophy unhindered by how to make it work. The Republican Congress now does that; and Ron Paul has done that in the past. Senators like Rand Paul wield much more power than Congressmen like Ron Paul, and hence Rand Paul is less free to express his philosophy.

Our summary issue stances below account for Rand Paul's bill sponsorships vs. Ron Paul's, as well as their political philosophy expressed in speeches out of the context of bills:

Where Rand Paul and Ron Paul agree on Foreign Policy issues

- Both oppose Iraq War
- Both oppose Cuban embargo
- Both agree on rights for Guantanamo detainees
- Both agree on non-intervention abroad
- Both oppose the TSA
- Both oppose the United Nations

Where Rand Paul and Ron Paul disagree on Foreign Policy issues

	Ron Paul	Rand Paul
Iran:	Stay out of Iran	Keep options on Iran
Israel:	Cut off all aid	Maintain alliance
Privacy vs. National Security:	Privacy first against terrorism	Spying on terrorists ok
Foreign aid:	End foreign aid	Limit foreign aid
Military Spending:	Cut absolute defense spending	Cut relative defense spending

Rand Paul vs. Jeb Bush on VoteMatch

Rand Paul and Jeb Bush disagree on many issues, but agree on some key stances as well: we discuss those summary agreements and disagreements in this final chapter.

Our "VoteMatch" quiz summarizes political views by analyzing responses to 20 questions below. Answers to the 20 questions are further summarized into a political philosophy, based on segregating the questions into a social axis and an economic axis (graphic on back cover; more detailed discussion below). That two-dimensional analysis concludes:

- *Rand Paul is a Conservative-Leaning Libertarian* (not a libertarian by the definition of the Libertarian Party; Rand Paul has many more conservative views than the Party). We comment in other chapters that he is more libertarian than the Tea Party (see p. 214), and certainly more libertarian than any other Republicans running in the 2016 primary.

- *Jeb Bush is a populist-leaning conservative* (not a libertarian like Rand Paul, and not a hard-core conservative like George W. Bush, but also not a moderate conservative like their father). Hard-core conservatives are well-represented in the 2016 GOP primary!

Where do Rand and Jeb disagree on the issues? They disagree on the core libertarian-versus-populist list, which focuses on differences in domestic policy like criminal prosecution and foreign policy like the use of the armed forces:

- *Crime:* Jeb supports the death penalty while Rand does not.

- *Marijuana:* Jeb supports the War on Drugs while Rand does not.

- *Military:* Jeb supports robust spending while Rand does not.

- *Iran:* Jeb supports intervention while Rand does not.

- *Cuba:* Jeb supports the embargo while Rand does not.

- *Environment:* Jeb supports EPA action while Rand does not.

Where do Rand and Jeb agree on the issues? Rand and Jeb agree on the core issues of the conservative economic agenda, including:

- *Tax policy:* both support cutting personal income taxes.

- *Corporate policy:* both support cutting corporate taxes.

- *Stimulus spending:* both support markets over federal stimulus.

- *Balanced Budget:* both support mandating limits on deficits.

- *School policy:* both support increasing parental choice.

What about social issues? Rand and Jeb agree on several core issues of the conservative social agenda, including:

- *Abortion policy:* both are pro-life.

- *Affirmative Action:* both oppose quotas.

- *Separating church and state:*
  both support God in the public sphere.

The most important agreement between Rand and Jeb is on immigration, where they both oppose the Republican Party line. Rand and Jeb both support comprehensive immigration reform with rights for guest workers and a path to citizenship. That issue is where other Republicans will challenge both Rand and Jeb; see our other books in this series for that discussion!

Rand Paul vs. Jeb Bush on VoteMatch

VoteMatch is our 20-question quiz which summarizes the candidate's views on the controversial issues of the day. The 20 questions appear on the left, with our summary answers for Rand and Jeb.

VoteMatch Social Issues

	Rand Paul	Jeb Bush
Abortion is a woman's unrestricted right	strongly opposes	strongly opposes
Legally require hiring women & minorities	opposes	opposes
Comfortable with same-sex marriage	opposes	strongly opposes
Keep God in the public sphere	strongly favors	strongly favors
Vouchers for school choice	strongly favors	strongly favors

VoteMatch Domestic Issues

	Rand Paul	Jeb Bush
Expand ObamaCare	strongly opposes	opposes
No 'rights' to clean air and water	strongly favors	strongly opposes
Stricter punishment reduces crime	strongly opposes	strongly favors
Absolute right to gun ownership	strongly favors	favors
Never legalize marijuana	strongly opposes	strongly favors

VoteMatch Economic Issues

	Rand Paul	Jeb Bush
Privatize Social Security	favors	mixed opinion
Higher taxes on the wealthy	strongly opposes	strongly opposes
More enforcement of the right to vote	strongly favors	strongly opposes
Stimulus better than market-led recovery	opposes	opposes
Prioritize green energy	strongly opposes	opposes

VoteMatch International Issues

	Rand Paul	Jeb Bush
Pathway to citizenship for illegal aliens	favors	favors
Support & expand free trade	strongly favors	favors
Maintain US sovereignty from UN	mixed opinion	opposes
Expand the military	opposes	favors
Stay out of Iran	strongly favors	opposes

In our online quiz, you fill in your answers for these 20 questions, and we match you against all the candidates (including Jeb and Rand and a dozen other contenders from both parties). Please see:

http://quiz.ontheissues.org/

Afterword

We hope that this book encourages you, as voters, to make your decisions based on the issues. We recognize the reality of American politics: voters make their decisions based primarily on whether they like the candidates. Accordingly, our goal is to get voters to compare their issue preferences in comparison to candidate issue stances when considering which candidates to like.

We intentionally omitted from this book any biographical background on Senator Paul and Governor Bush. Details of their birthplaces and religious affiliations — and minutiae of every other personal detail — are readily available in the mainstream media. Their issue stances are more challenging for voters to find.

Why does the mainstream media fail at this important function? Because they are "news" organizations which are poorly suited to covering political campaigns. "News" implies reporting on what is "new": Jeb's stance on criminal sentencing has not changed since 2010, and Rand's stance on abortion has not changed, ever, so there's nothing in the news about those issues. But if you are impassioned about Three Strikes, or if you vote based on pro-life vs. pro-choice stances, then you cannot rely on the news media for those non-newsworthy issues. And that's where we come in.

This book represents an archive of where these two candidates stand on the key issues of our time. We don't consider whether candidates' issue stances are new — just what they say on each issue. That often requires a lot of digging on our part — we have a team of researchers to do that, but we invite you to volunteer any issue stances that we don't cover.

Our online website www.ontheissues.org covers many more issues than can fit in any book: many more stances from Jeb Bush and Rand Paul, as well as all of the other 2016 candidates, Governors, Senators, and House members. We score each candidate on a 20-question quiz called "VoteMatch." A representation of the VoteMatch quiz results for the presidential contenders appears on the back cover of this book. The mainstream media interpret candidates using a one-dimensional "right-left" analysis. That simplistic analysis comes to nonsensical conclusions like calling Rand Paul "extreme right-wing" even though he opposed the Iraq War and supports marijuana decriminalization.

We find our two-dimensional analysis to be more accurate in differentiating candidates than that traditional one-dimensional analysis. We don't claim that our method is perfect — just superior to the simplistic mainstream media. VoteMatch uses a Social Issues dimension plus an Economic Issues dimension; we interpret candidates based on whether they believe in government involvement in either or both of those dimensions. Using the two-dimensional analysis differentiates five classes of political beliefs:

1. *Libertarian:*
   No government involvement in social issues
   No government involvement in economic issues

2. *Conservative:*
   Government involvement in social issues
   No government involvement in economic issues

3. *Liberal:*
   No government involvement in social issues
   Government involvement in economic issues

4. *Populist:*
   Government involvement in social issues
   Government involvement in economic issues

5. *Centrist:*
   Some government involvement in social issues
   Some government involvement in economic issues

Most importantly, you can answer the same 20 questions and see *your* political label and how the candidates match up with *you*. We invite you to try the VoteMatch quiz at:

http://quiz.ontheissues.org

Index

Bosch, Orlando: 165
Brady Campaign: 13
Brazil: 163,191
Brown, Scott: 210
Budget deficit: 52-3
Budget, Federal: 51, 54, 130, 161
Burnham Institute: 115
Bush, George H. W.: 43, 71, 154, 165, 200, 204, 219, 221-3, 225, 228
Bush, George W.: 26, 72-3, 105-6, 115, 141, 159, 169-70, 185, 189,
    192, 200, 210, 216, 219, 221-8, 234

C

Cain, Herman: 140
California: 19, 22, 25, 115
Campaign finance: 43, 55, 64-5
Canada: 58, 66, 191
Cap and Trade: 174, 176
Capital gains: 68
Capital punishment *see:* Death penalty
Carbon emissions: 176-7
Castro, Fidel: 164-5
Catholic Church: 125,133, 225
Central Intelligence Agency (CIA): 150, 158, 165
Character: 111, 117, 123, 133, 225, 229-30
Chavez, Hugo: 192-3
Chemical weapons: 147
Children: 14, 80-1, 96-9, 107, 122-7,129, 133, 204
Chiles, Lawton: 17, 113, 129
Chile: 191
China: 52, 86, 128,153, 182,188-9,191
Christian: 60, 110, 122, 128-9,132-3,204   *see also:* Catholic Church
Christie, Chris: 26, 169, 204
Chrysler: 47, 61
Citizenship: 171, 194-6, 198-9, 205, 235, 237
Civil union: 119, 121
A Clear Vision to Revitalize America, by Rand Paul (2013):
    102, 104, 148, 190
    Book review: 202
Climate change: 170-1, 174-5,
Climate Change Treaty *see:* Kyoto Accord
Clinton, Bill: 118-9
Clinton, Hillary: 139-40, 148, 162, 164-5, 215, 225
Cold War: 46, 168, 183
College *see:* University
Common Core: 73, 92-3
Comprehensive Everglades Restoration Plan: 29, 43
Confederate flag: 131, 220 *also see:* Flag

Congressional Budget Office (CBO): 161
Conservative Political Action Conference (CPAC): 103, 121, 130, 136, 201
Constitution: *see:* US Constitution, Florida Constitution
Contraception *see:* Birth control
Corporate regulation: 46-7
Corporate welfare: 42, 48-9, 230
Creationism: 111
Crime: 8, 13-9, 21-2, 144, 195, 197, 228, 230, 236
Crime rate: 15, 17
Crimea: 168
Crist, Charlie: 41, 101, 201
Cruz, Ted: 3, 137, 214
Cuba: 140-1,163-5, 179, 219, 233-4
Cubana Airlines: 165

D

Death penalty: 8, 18-9, 36, 219
Death tax: *see:* Taxes
Debt ceiling: 53, 208
Defense: 162-3 *see also:* US Department of Defense
   Spending: 160-1
Defense of Marriage Act (DOMA): 106, 116, 118, 121
   see also: Gay Rights
DeMint, Jim: 54, 201, 208-9
Democratic party: 3,8-9,36-7,41-2,47,51,53,62,7-8,102,
   120-1,125,133, 150-1, 162, 178, 183, 209
Department of Children and Families: 127
Department of Energy (DOE): 31, 161
Disabilities: 127
Discrimination: 88, 117, 121
DNA (deoxyribonucleic acid) testing: 18, 180
Domestic violence: 13
Don't Ask, Don't Tell (DADT): 118 *see:* Gay Rights
Drug cartels: 21, 193
Drugs, illegal: 20-1

E

Ebola: 186-7
Economy: 50-5
Education: 79, 80, 92-9, 225, 230
   see also: Common Core, No Child Left Behind, University
Education savings accounts: 99
Egypt: 128, 130, 157
El Salvador: 189
Eminent domain: 57
Employ American Workers Act: 85

G

Gangs: 21, 111
Gates, Robert: 162
Gay marriage: 106, 116, 119, 121,   *see also:* Gay rights
Gay rights: 106, 116-7, 225, 230
Gaza: 157
General Motors: 47,61
GLBT *see:* Gay Rights
God: 132,181, 235-6
Goldman-Sachs: 64
Goldwater Institute: 99
GOP *see:* Republican Party
Government Bullies, by Sen. Rand Paul (2012): 28, 42, 56, 144, 182
  Book review: 207
Government downsizing: 163
Great Recession *see:* Recession
Gulf of Mexico: 59
Gun control: 8, 12-3,   *see also:* gun crimes, 2nd Amendment
Gun crimes: 14-5
Gun rights *see:* 2nd Amendment

H

Hamas: 157
Healthcare *see:* Medicaid, Medicare, Mental health, ObamaCare
Heller decision: 12
Hezbollah: 147
High School: 89, 90-1, 93-4
Hispanic: 41, 47, 89, 124-5, 196, 203-5, 219
Homosexuality: *see:* Gay Rights
Hourly wage: 87
House of Representatives Bills:
  H.Con.Res.25 (2007): 61
  H.R.1091 (2011): 114
Hurricanes: 9, 26-7, 219

I

Illegal immigrants: 171, 194-9, 203-6
Immigration: 124, 126, 198-9
Immigration Wars, by Jeb Bush (2013):
  4, 21, 47, 85, 97, 99, 125, 135, 193, 195
  Book review: 203
India: 149, 153
Inheritance tax: 43, 68-9   *also see:* Taxes

Insurance
  Unemployment insurance: 72, 86, 104
  Health insurance: 76-9, 116
  Malpractice insurance: 82-3
International Atomic Energy Agency (IAEA): 152
International Diplomacy: 169, 184
Internet: 9, 32-5, 122, 190
Internet Freedom Preservation Act: 32
Iowa: 110, 112
Iran: 37,141, 147, 166, 182, 215
  Sanctions: 152-4
  Nuclear Weapons in: 152,-3 160
Iraq: 128, 146, 153, 160-1, 215, 231,
Iraq War: 141, 154-5, 159, 170, 179, 233, 239
ISIL (Islamic State in Iraq and the Levant) *see:* ISIS
ISIS (Islamic State in Iraq and Syria): 140-1, 146-7, 155, 179, 183
Islam: 133, 144, 150, 162
  Shia-Sunni: 147, 154, 162
Israel: 37, 141, 153, 156-7, 163, 166, 183, 185, 233

J

Japan: 66, 155, 163, 191
Jews: 156, 169, 185
Jinping, Xi: 189
Jobs: 46, 66, 72, 84-9
  Creation: 87
  Growth: 87

K

King, Martin Luther: 26, 117
Korea: 166-7
  Korea, North: 141, 153, 166, 215
  Korea, South: 155, 163, 167, 191
Kosovo: 163
Kuwait: 154-5
Kyoto Treaty: 176-7

L

Labor standards: 190
Latin America: 37, 192-3
Latino *see:* Hispanic
Levant: 146 *also see:* ISIL
Libertarian party: 3, 8-9, 138, 170, 210-2, 234, 255
Libya: 128, 162
Lu, Annette: 189

M

Management Privatization Act: 63
Mandatory prison sentences *see:* Prison incarceration
Marijuana, legalization: 20, 22-3, 234, 236, 238
Marriage: 120-3 *see also:* Gay marriage
Martin, Trayvon: 13
Mass transit: 9, 24-5 *see also:* Transportation infrastructure
McCain, John: 51, 64-5, 159, 204, 210-1
Medical doctor: *see:* Physicians
Medical malpractice: 82-3   *also see:* Insurance, Malpractice
Medical marijuana *see:* Marijuana, legalization
Medicare/Medicaid: 51-2, 72, 78-9, 220
Mental health care: 80-1
Mexico: 48, 140, 191, 193, 204
Mexico border: 21, 192-3
Miami: 13, 191
Middle East: 37, 128, 141, 147, 152-9, 162-3
Military: *see:* US Department of Defense
Military Bases: *see: Base Realignment and Closure*
Minnesota: 22, 96
Morality: 134-5, 231
Mortgage Bankers Association: 55
Mortgages: 55, 68
Muslim: *see:* Islam
My Father, My President, by Doro Bush Koch (2006): Book review: 221

N

National Governors Association (NGA): 33, 177
National Guard: 12, 21, 140, 181, 193
National gun registry: 178
National Rifle Association (NRA): 13
National security: 37, 52, 140-1, 158, 184, 233
NATO: 183, 185,
Nazis: 111
New Hampshire: 22
New York state (NY): 22, 26
New York City (NYC): 25-6
Newborn: 127
Newtown, Connecticut shootings: 14
Nixon, Richard M.: 213
No Child Left Behind (NCLB): 72, 94-5
No Place Like Home: 127
Non-violent criminal offenders: 22
Norquist, Grover: 53, 70-1
North America Free-Trade Agreement (NAFTA): 171, 191

Now or Never, by Sen. Jim DeMint (2012): 54, 201
    Book review: 208
Nuclear Non-Proliferation Treaty: 152
Nuclear power: 30-1, 60 *see also:* Energy policy
Nuclear waste: 30 *see also:* Yucca Mountain
Nuclear weapons: 31, 150, 160-1, 166

O

Obama, Barack: 24-6, 31-2, 46, 52, 54, 86, 90, 94, 102, 115-6, 126,
    130, 137, 140, 147, 150, 154, 158, 161, 164-5, 167, 169, 171, 179,
    181, 183, 186-7, 203-4, 209, 215, 224,
Obama Administration: 58, 92, 149, 153, 159, 193,
ObamaCare: 49-50, 72, 76-8, 81, 228, 232, 236,
Office of the Governor: 105
Oil drilling: 58-60, 228
Oman: 163
Open government: 37, 255
Organized labor *see:* Unions

P

Palin, Sarah: 140, 156, 204, 210, 224, 226
Palestine: 146, 156-7,
Palestinian Liberation Organization (PLO): 157
Parental notification: 113 *also see:* Abortion
Partisanship: 107, 136-7
Patriot Act: 9, 12, 14, 36
Paul, Ron: 213-5, 231-3
Pentagon: 118, 151, 160-3
Philosophy: 4, 9, 63, 73, 101, 107, 212, 215-6, 231-3, 234
Physicians: 110, 134, 192
Police: 13, 16, 19-20, 150, 194
Political Action Committees (PAC): 43, 64, 157, 209
Poor: 46, 48, 79, 98, 102-3, 167, 192
Pregnancy: 19, 113
Principles: 134-5, 184-5
Prison incarceration: 16-7, 23
Prisons: 8, 15-8, 22-3, 36-7, 101, 164-5, 207,
Privacy: 127, 145, 226, 233
Privatization: 62-3, 73, 91,100-1, 216, 220
Pro-choice: 113, 238 *see also:* Abortion
Profiles in Character, by Jeb Bush (1996):
    49, 103, 107, 111, 117, 123, 133
    Book review: 229
Project for a New American Century (PNAC): 169, 170
Progressive wing: 37, 100, 106, 214-5, 223   *also see:* Democratic party
Pro-life: 113, 115, 122, 211, 225, 235, 238 *see also:* Abortion

Protect IP Act (PIPA): 34
Public schools: 96-7, 99, 129

R

Race to the Top: 92
Reagan, Ronald: 28, 30, 71, 134, 137, 160, 184, 222-3
Recession, Great: 42, 47, 50-1, 72, 188
Religion: 107, 128-9, 132-3, 225
Religious right: 3, 106-7, 114, 201
Renewable energy: *see:* Alternative energy
Reproductive rights: *see:* Pro-choice *see also:* Abortion
Republican Jewish Coalition: 156, 169, 185
Republican Party: 3, 8, 16, 19, 41-3, 66, 71, 73, 87, 100, 106, 111,
    120, 124-5, 136-7, 164, 169, 185, 197-8, 203-5, 209-10, 214-7, 234-5
Roe v. Wade: 113 *also see:* Abortion, *see also:* Pro-choice
Romney, Mitt: 51,159,169, 203-4, 224
Ryan, Paul: 51, 78, 137
Rubio, Marco: 91, 101, 116, 134, 137, 164, 201, 204-5, 210, 214
Russia: 37, 141, 168-9, 179, 185

S

Salazar, Joe: 61
Same-sex marriage: *see:* Gay marriage
Sandy Hook Elementary School *see:* Newtown, Connecticut
SAT: 89
Saudi Arabia: 37,147, 149, 154, 158, 163
Scholastic Aptitude Test (SAT) see: SAT
School prayer: 107, 129
School vouchers: 73, 85, 94, 97-9, 225, 236
Schools
    Charter: 95-7, 230
    Parochial: 97
    Private: 97, 99
    Public: 96-7, 99, 129
Scripps Medical Institute: 115, 230
Secrecy, government: 9, 36-7, 152
Secretary of State: 148

Other Books in This Series

Acknowledgments

This book would not have been possible without the tireless efforts of the entire OnTheIssues team: Nicholai Alexandrovich (our indexer), Jay Camara, Derek Camara (our cover artist), Janice Gordon, Michele Gordon, Joshua Hoerr (our App designer), Marissa Hoerr (our Facebook consultant), Peter Hoerr, Ram Lau, Rachael Lawrence, Jamie Leighton, Naomi Lichtenberg, Ogden Porter, Will Rico, Dan Teittinen, Irma Teittinen, and especially Kathleen Camara.

About the Editor

Jesse Gordon has been the editor-in-chief of OnTheIssues.org since its formation in 1999. His passion revolves around providing issue-based coverage on political races, to combat the mainstream media's growing lack of such coverage.

Mr. Gordon holds a Master's degree in Public Policy from Harvard University's Kennedy School of Government. He and the website OnTheIssues.org are based in Cambridge, Massachusetts. He resides with his fiancée, Kathleen; his son Julien; Kathleen's son Derek; their cat Chanel; and four fish with whom Chanel is obsessed.

Mr. Gordon's politics are, on the VoteMatch chart, a libertarian-leaning progressive (upper left quadrant). He is a registered Independent, but has voted for Democrats, Republicans, Greens, and Libertarians. He was the founder of both the Progressive Democrats of Cambridge, and the Harvard University Libertarian Caucus. His most important political values are open government, as reflected in the open issues concept underlying the OnTheIssues website.

Mr. Gordon replies to email personally, at jesse@ontheissues.org — whether to suggest improvements to the website or to order one of the other books above.

www.ingramcontent.com/pod-product-compliance
Lightning Source LLC
Chambersburg PA
CBHW050439290526
45786CB00006B/2082